FIGHTING IT OUT

FIGHTING IT OUT

*When Bulgaria's greatest entrepreneur
comes home, he finds a snake-pit
at his country's heart...*

Atanas Tilev

STACEY INTERNATIONAL

Fighting it Out

published by
Stacey International
128 Kensington Church Street
London W8 4BH
Fax: 020 7792 9288
E-mail: stacey.international@virgin.net

© Atanas Tilev 2001

Atanas Tilev asserts the moral right to be
identified as the author of this work

A catalogue record for this book is
available from the British Library

ISBN 1 900988 38 0

Printed and bound by Tien Wah Press, Singapore

This book is sold subject to the condition that it shall not, by way of trade or otherwise, be lent, re-sold, hired out or otherwise circulated without the publisher's prior consent in any form of binding or cover other than that in which it is published and without a similar condition including this condition being imposed by the subsequent purchaser.

All rights reserved. No part of this publication may be reproduced, stored in a retrieval system, or transmitted in any form or by any means, electronic, mechanical, photocopying, recording or otherwise, without the prior permission of the publisher.

To my mother - with a bow

ACKNOWLEDGEMENTS

But for a few true friends who, regardless of the danger to themselves, saved my life, I would not be around to tell my story. To them goes my boundless gratitude.

A great many people in different ways played their part in the birth of this book. Throughout my life, and in the creation of this work, they have helped me. They are too numerous to mention, but they know who they are.

I thank my dear children for their understanding and support during some of the most hazardous years of my life.

My most special thanks go to my beloved R for her unceasing support throughout the creation and realisation of this book.

AT September 2001

CONTENTS

1.	Introduction	
3.	Chapter One :	*The Escape*
17.	Chapter Two :	*A Happy Childhood beneath Dark Clouds*
27.	Chapter Three :	*The Chosen Ones*
43.	Chapter Four :	*Love from a Cold Climate*
59.	Chapter Five :	*Entering a Different World*
77.	Chapter Six :	*Conquering Russia*
95.	Chapter Seven :	*Conquering the Far East*
105.	Chapter Eight :	*A Complete Idiot*
111.	Chapter Nine :	*Treachery Afoot*
119.	Chapter Ten :	*His Royal Highness, King Simeon II*
123.	Chapter Eleven:	*Killing my Baby*
131.	Chapter Twelve :	*Down and Out in Milan*
139.	Chapter Thirteen :	*Meanwhile, Back in Bulgaria*
145.	Chapter Fourteen:	*The Great National Robbery*
171.	Chapter Fifteen :	*The Destruction of the Banks*
185.	Chapter Sixteen :	*'Mr Tilev Must be Hit'*
190.	Chapter Seventeen :	*So What Now?*

INTRODUCTION

I was surely born with the ancient Chinese curse – that I would 'live in interesting times'.

This book is about the many twists and turns in my life so far. Alas, it is also about how many of the dreams one believes to have come true so easily turn into mere *fata morgana*.

Much of the story you are about to read concerns the former Communist Party in Bulgaria, which led and crippled the country and the Bulgarian people for forty-five years and which after the collapse of communism turned itself into a criminal governmental junta bent on robbing and ravaging the country ever further.

When I returned to Bulgaria in 1993 it was with brave intentions. I abominated everything about communism and what it had done to my country throughout my lifetime, and I was determined to do whatever I could to help my people rebuild their lives and heal the wounds inflicted upon them. I returned having succeeded in earning a private fortune in the West. Yet I was a relative innocent, truly unable to believe that the plot unfurling around me was real. It took me two years fully to understand the enormity and complexity of the robbery of the national wealth that had been carried out under the noses of the Bulgarian people.

Let the reader not misinterpret those events and developments of my business career I find myself obliged to cite in the narrative, as the consequence of my warped view of the scene around or my complete idiocy. I tell of them to illustrate both the salient turning points of my professional life and how hard-won my disillusionment was. Thankfully, even now, my positive business experiences far outnumber the negative ones.

The grim ground of my personal experience on returning to Bulgaria has now seen a radical change towards hope for better things, in these few months since the sweeping parliamentary victory of my friend King Simeon II, in early 2001. At last my home country has a real chance of laying the foundations of normal, prospering, European nationhood, with government by law and the leadership of a man meeting the highest standards of probity and competence such as the task demands. The phenomenon of a king offering himself for election and becoming prime minister is in itself unprecedented. It may now be that Bulgaria will have pulled off a feat of reform in a manner not hitherto recorded in the history of mankind.

Atanas Tilev 2001

CHAPTER ONE

THE ESCAPE

As the car skidded to a halt I pulled my pistol from under my designer suit and passed it across to the last of the bodyguards sitting beside me. He nodded his understanding and slid the gun into his pocket. Neither of us said a word. He had run with me to this car from the armour-plated BMW and the rest of the convoy. He and the gun were the last protection I had.

Once I left this car I would be on my own.

I climbed out and the heat hit me like a mallet. I started walking, my heart thumping and the perspiration already breaking through, not looking back as I heard the car accelerating away. If they got me now I would have no way of defending myself, no back door to escape through. One of the greatest lessons in life, and in business, is never to get into any situation unless you can see a way out should you need it. Now there was no way out; I had to keep going and just hope the plan worked.

If I had arrived in this world one month earlier I would have been born a free man; as it was this was the second time I had left Bulgaria. The first time had been through luck rather than planning and had happened at the end of my childhood. And now in 1996 I was escaping again, on foot in thirty-five-

Fighting it Out

degree heat. I was one of the richest men in the country but if I did not succeed in getting past the border guards without being recognised I would be dead; or imprisoned without trial, which would be as good as dead, possibly worse. I had uncovered one of the biggest crimes ever planned and the perpetrators were determined to silence me. The word had gone out: 'Mr Tilev must be hit.' They were powerful people with tentacles everywhere and they stood to lose billions of dollars if their plans failed.

I was one kilometre from the border and wished I was still armed. But if I was going to mingle with the locals crossing back and forth on foot, I couldn't afford to be caught with a pistol tucked into the belt of my business suit. I missed the sensation of having it there; the gun had made me feel a little safer in the months I'd been carrying it. If all other precautions had failed I would still have been able to defend myself against attack, but now I was defenceless. There were plenty of people in Bulgaria who wanted to see an end to me. It costs very little to hire an assassin in a country run by criminals.

Not that it would have been easy for a killer to have taken a clear shot at me during the previous two years. From the moment the death threats started and I told my friend, a general in the army, that I felt I and my elder daughter needed protection, we had been guarded round the clock. A force of sixty men, all giants and members of the special forces, had been deployed to look after us. An armoured BMW 750 limousine had been imported to replace the conspicuous red BMW 850 I had been driving before.

'Are you mad?' my friends had wanted to know when they saw me driving around in the unprotected sports car. 'You could be dragged from the driving seat and murdered at any set of traffic lights!' Until that moment it had never occurred to me I would come to any harm in Bulgaria. It was the country of my birth, after all, a country supposed now to be freed from repression. Why should I be afraid? But after the threats, everywhere I went I had two guards in the car, as well as the driver, and travelled in a convoy with two jeeps, one in front and one behind, carrying four more armed men in each. Going to work each day had become a circus. That was how I had set out from home that morning, driving fast to try and lose the counter-intelligence agents who were following us, carrying the warrant for my arrest, which this time had been signed by all the right people.

The agents stayed close to us as we came down out of the mountains towards the city. My drivers all knew that we had to lose them, that this was my last chance to stay a free man, but that didn't mean they would succeed in time for the rendezvous with the other car that we hoped was waiting for us. Eventually we pulled far enough ahead to be able to get out of sight. We had no more than a few seconds to make the switch before the counter-intelligence men rounded the bend behind us. The car was waiting, the engine turning over, the driver's fingers tight on the steering wheel.

I threw open the door of the BMW and ran across with my bodyguard beside me, his eyes darting around in search of a sniper's barrel. We hurled ourselves onto the back seat of the waiting car. The man who had been hiding on the floor of the BMW sat up to take my place and the convoy sped on its way. As the counter-intelligence people appeared over the horizon after the convoy, we drove away towards the chosen border crossing in a modest family saloon.

In the end it hadn't been the contract on my life that had forced me to flee. That I had dealt with in my usual direct manner, tracking down the hired killer and making it clear it would not be in his family's interests to murder me. I would never have been able to carry out the threat; I had no idea who his family were, let alone where they lived, but people judge you by their

Fighting it Out

own standards. He would happily have murdered my family, so he was quick to believe I would do the same to him. Nor had it been the two official-looking death sentences that had been sent to me. More frightening had been the news that yet another warrant had been issued for my arrest, this time signed by the highest of authorities within Bulgarian counter-intelligence. I could guard myself against an assassin and I could fight against the death threats, but there was nothing I could do if the police came to arrest me with all the official papers signed and sealed.

I knew that if I was brought to trial I would be acquitted and my accusers disgraced, but how long would I be left to rot in a prison cell before that trial came about? What deprivations and tortures would I be forced to endure before they acquitted me and charmingly invited me to walk free? At the very least it would be months, and during those months they would be more than able to ruin my mind and my life, incarcerating me with the most dangerous of criminals and questioning me day and night for as long as it took to break my will and force me to confess to some ludicrous charge. They could accuse me of spying for the Iranians and I would have a hard time proving them liars. I was under no illusion that I was any different to the millions of other people who have been destroyed in this way by oppressive regimes. No amount of wealth or influence can help a man held in jail by people who have no conscience and don't care about the consequences of their actions. It was also extremely likely that if I were arrested I would end up being shot in the back, 'while trying to escape', one of the favourite official excuses for murder.

As the border crossing came into view I wiped the sweat from my brow. Everything looked quiet, the modest building baking quietly in the heat, the guards listlessly going about their duties. My jacket was over my shoulder and I had loosened my tie, but my shirt was still soaked through. I took

The Escape

a moment to survey the scene, aware that if I stood for too long I would risk drawing attention to myself. There were a number of workers walking back and forth past the booth, the guards checking their papers with looks of indifference. I knew I was too well groomed and smartly dressed to pass as a local on his way to work; I would need a cover story. The odd car was being flagged down by armed soldiers, the occupants carefully scrutinised and the number plates noted down. Being on foot was the right choice. If I'd arrived here in my own car I would have stuck out like a sore thumb amongst the elderly battered vehicles which most people had to drive, and I didn't want the friend who had lent me his car to have the number plate noted down anywhere where investigators could dig it up once they discovered I had escaped from the country.

As I sauntered up towards the booth I tried to assess whether the guards seemed to be looking for anyone in particular. With any luck the authorities still had no idea that I knew a warrant was out for my arrest. Hopefully, they would have had no reason to provide the border guards with my photograph, but the guards might still recognise my face from the television. It had been on the news bulletins almost every night for months. A friend who bore a reasonable resemblance to me had given me his passport and if I got through to the other side my first task would be to burn it so he would never be linked to my escape. If the guard just glanced quickly he would see a bad photograph of a younger man. I trusted he would assume it was an old picture of me.

There were two or three people standing at the window, waiting to be allowed through. They turned to look at me, obviously surprised to see a man in expensive clothes leaving the country on foot.

'My bloody car broke down,' I grumbled, loudly enough for the guard inside the booth to hear, 'just a kilometre down the road. I've left it with a mechanic. I'll have to pick it up

Fighting it Out

when I come back tonight.'

The official's bored eyes flicked up from the papers he was studying and stared at me blankly for a second. He snapped shut the passport in his hands and pushed it back to one of the men in front without a word. There were two more men in the front of me and he waved them through impatiently as they held up their passports for inspection.

'My car broke down,' I explained again as I passed over my friend's papers, taking out a handkerchief to mop my brow. If I seemed agitated, this story about a breakdown might help to explain it. The official couldn't have been less interested in my problems. There was a computer screen flickering beside him. Another guard who had been inspecting cars ambled over to join us.

'My car broke down,' I said yet again.

'A bad day to be on foot,' he said, gesturing at the sun which was burning down from a cloudless sky. 'Do you have far to go?'

'Not far,' I lied. 'Just to the village. I'll wait until the evening to come back. When it's cool.'

Casual conversation, normally so natural, became almost impossible with a dry throat and every nerve tensed. The two men exchanged looks that normally I would not have noticed. Two women had joined the queue behind me and a van full of vegetables drew up. The man in the booth gave me back my papers and the guard moved off to talk to the farmer in the van. I slipped the passport into my shirt pocket as nonchalantly as possible and strolled out of Bulgaria, expecting at any moment to hear a shout of recognition and a brusque order to return, or possibly even shots. There was a house surrounded by trees about two hundred metres up the road. I reckoned that once I was past the house I would be safe from gunfire and could afford to break into a run should anything go wrong.

It was the longest two hundred metres of my life. Sweat was

seeping from every pore in my skin as I forced myself to keep trudging on without looking back. There were others walking along the road as well, each preoccupied with the petty problems of surviving another day in a part of the world which takes any more ambitious thoughts out of the range of most people. All they saw when they looked at me was another businessman going about his work.

The small run-down house was drawing nearer. I could see some children chasing a goat around in the shade of the trees and a woman pegging out washing as she shouted at them. It was all so normal. I walked past and as the shade of the trees fell across me, I paused for a second in the cool and looked back for the first time. The border post had disappeared from sight. I was safe. All I had to do now was get myself to Vienna and start working out what to do next. I was confident that I had successfully exposed the men who had been conspiring to rob my country of every penny it had, but the damage done to the economy was still enormous and there was no one left in government or public life who had the will and the power to pull Bulgaria back from the brink of starvation. I had succeeded in foiling their plan and exposing them as criminals, but not in saving the banking system from collapse.

Standing at the side of the road, out of the sun, I stuck my thumb out at the passing traffic. The first van to come past drew up and the driver waited for me to climb in beside him. He offered me a cigarette and a can of lemonade. I accepted both, even though I normally only smoke cigars and then only after a good dinner. I needed to do something with my hands to stop them from shaking and the smoke would help to calm my nerves.

We exchanged a few pleasantries about the heat and about the state of the roads and then fell into a companionable silence. My main thoughts were for Maria, my elder daughter, who was still in Bulgaria. I had been trying to persuade her to leave the country and go back to her mother in Finland, but I

Fighting it Out

had had no success. How do you persuade a headstrong nineteen-year-old to leave her friends and boyfriend and a life she enjoys? I had tried to explain the danger to her, but she felt comfortable in Bulgaria, and saw no reason to go. Despite all the problems, it is a beautiful country and the Bulgarians are a warm charming people. I knew she would be well protected and there was little chance the authorities would try to arrest her now I had gone; even they would have trouble justifying the arrest of a schoolgirl. But I was still anxious. If they needed a way to get me to do as they wanted, she was the obvious target. I would have to think of some way to tempt her out of the country before it was too late.

The van driver was only going as far as the next small town, where we said goodbye over a cup of coffee in a café, and I set off once more with my thumb out, in search of another benefactor. By now my normally immaculate appearance was extremely tousled. I had abandoned my tie hours before and my shirt was sticking unpleasantly to my skin. I felt hot and dirty, impatient to be at the end of my journey and back in control of my life.

In a series of small hops in a succession of vans and cars, I made my way north towards Vienna, destroying my friend's passport on the way and reverting to my own identity as I finally reached the Austrian border, by which time I looked sufficiently dishevelled to attract the attention of the officials. But now I was almost home and dry. A phone call to my office in Vienna confirmed who I was and I was able to telephone for a car and driver to pick me up for the final leg of my journey to my Austrian home.

The troubles that my country had suffered since 1944, the year of my birth, had destroyed many families like mine. The fact that I had not been destroyed, merely forced to make a life for myself outside my native country, had been partly due to luck and partly to the legacy of my grandfather, a man who made sure that even in the darkest days of communist rule I was never fooled by the party line and was always aware of the truth.

The truth was that when the communists had marched south from Russia into Bulgaria, the intelligentsia, people like my grandfather, had had no idea that they would stay. They assumed that, once the war was over, the Russians would return north and the country would be free once more to trade and prosper as it always had done. How could they have known any different? How could they have known that a year later, in 1945, Churchill and Roosevelt would make a pact with Stalin at Yalta which would give our country to the communists for the next half century?

With that decision the leaders of the free world effectively signed Bulgaria off. By the time men like my grandfather realised what had happened the communists had sealed the borders as tightly as any prison. If they had not done so they would have seen half the population emigrate in their determination to escape the murderous tyranny of Stalin. The enslavement of the Bulgarian people had begun.

A month after the communists arrived my mother, Irina, gave birth to me. Apparently, when I emerged into the world, I was covered in a film of tallow. 'This boy will not be like the others!' the midwife announced to my mother. 'Only one child in a hundred thousand has such a thing happen to them.'

Irina, like all new mothers, was hungry for any sign that her first child might be in some way marked out for greatness and decided at that moment that no stone would be left unturned in my education, no skill left unhoned, no potential left untapped, no opportunity for improvement left unexplored. In most ways I was an eager recipient of her plans for my improvement; by the age of ten I had learned the Iliad by heart. She was like a bulldozer travelling through my childhood ahead of me, clearing every obstacle from my path; my father, Jeko, stood back and watched, a cold, stubborn and

Fighting it Out

introverted man.

Before the communists marched south and seized every piece of private land and property on behalf of the state, both sides of my family had enjoyed a prosperity and respect earned by many generations. To the communists that meant nothing. Everything was taken away; their lands, their work, their money. My paternal grandfather was a substantial land and mill owner, but everything went overnight. From being rich and secure my family became poor at the stroke of a pen.

All my maternal grandfather, a distinguished architect, builder and businessman who had studied in Germany, was allowed to keep was his family home in Stara Zagora, at least for a while, and that was where I was brought up. It was a big house, one of the nicest in the city. We even managed to keep a few servants, although they had to be gypsies because we could no longer afford to pay Bulgarians. Stara Zagora had once been the capital of one of the Thracian provinces and had a proud history. Men like my grandfather were not likely to have their spirit crushed overnight.

In the evenings, when he and Grandma were not out visiting, my grandfather would invite his friends round to talk, drink and play cards. They had been the cream of Stara Zagora society: the architects, lawyers, doctors and dentists, the brave and distinguished members of the opposition party, including their leader 'Gemeto', the great Georgi Dimitrov, who was head of the Agrarian Party and a sworn enemy of the communists.

Before they arrived I would secrete myself beneath the table, hidden by the folds of my grandmother's linen tablecloth, so that I could eavesdrop on their conversations. Often, because of the frequent power cuts, the room was lit by flickering candles. They all talked five or six languages and would exchange information about what Truman or Eisenhower had said, discussing their hopes that sooner or

The Escape

later the Soviet Union would be destroyed and there would be an end to the deadening hand of communism in our country. Although they were mostly old men who had the best of their lives behind them, they were still brave to express such opinions out loud. One by one they disappeared mysteriously and only years later did we find out, when some of them returned as shadows of their former selves, where they had been taken to. There had been no trials, apart from the occasional show trial, just a knock on the door in the middle of the night and a brusque order to put on a shirt and go.

Anyone who was suspected of being brighter or better educated than those around him was taken away to a concentration camp and worked and starved until either they died or their spirit was destroyed. Some of them were shot while 'trying to escape'. As I grew up, listening to and watching everything that went on around me, all the most gifted and talented people of the generations before me were murdered. The moral fibre of the country was systematically destroyed in a genocide every bit as cruel and merciless and stupid as that which would later come to places like Cambodia and Rwanda. It was happening all over the Soviet Union and Eastern Europe; millions of the best people being killed so that the mediocre could rise safely to the top. It was the only way that the system could be made to work because intelligent people ask questions and argue.

My grandfather gave me a great deal of attention even though the authorities forced him to work in Yambol, which meant he had to commute great distances and only came home for two days a week. We would take long walks together in the countryside and he would ask what nonsense I had been taught at school about history and literature. I'd tell him and he would explain how my teachers were distorting the truth in order to give us the party line. Without his balancing influence I would have believed what I was taught in school and heard

Fighting it Out

on the radio, simply because there was no alternative; I would have heard nothing else from the cradle. But I was confused by the different messages from the grown-ups around me. No one was allowed to question the system openly, because once you start to question communism the whole system collapses. While the simple premise of equality was easy to sell to the many millions who lived in poverty, it was impossible to make it work without repression.

My grandfather used to listen to Radio Free Europe, only able to catch the odd few words and phrases through the static of the communist jamming devices. He made me aware that there was a very different world outside the borders of Bulgaria. If I had not had him to guide me I would never have known there was an alternative to the information we were all being force-fed. I would have believed that communism could provide paradise on earth for all of us and, as an ambitious and able young man, I would almost certainly have followed a career in the party, as many of my friends went on to do. The only path to success within the country was to join the system. But my grandfather told me that there were alternatives.

'Everything they are teaching you is propaganda,' he would explain. 'Think about the things they are telling you and ask yourself if you believe that any of it can be true?' Then he would explain the way things really were. I knew he was telling the truth, but I also knew that when I wasn't inside the safe confines of the family home I had to behave like everyone else. I had to listen to the lies and pretend to believe them. The only alternatives were death or a labour camp.

My grandfather had two brothers who had been communists before the Russians invaded, at a time when the idea of equality for all was very attractive to many rebellious young intellectuals. At that time Grandad also had a friend, Colonel Pantchev, who was in charge of the local army division. Whenever an action was planned against the communists, Pantchev would warn Grandad, who would then warn his brothers. When the Russians arrived, Pantchev was prosecuted by the so-called People's Court in the local theatre, accused of persecuting communists. Grandad was the only man brave enough to stand up in front of everyone and tell of Pantchev's valour, but he could not save his friend. Pantchev was shot 'attempting to escape'. Both my grandfather's brothers threw away their party membership cards during collectivisation.

By the time the Russians arrived, my grandfather was an elderly man; he could afford to stand by his principles. Maybe he would have stuck to his principles anyway, but it would have been harder if he had had a young family to support and protect. It also helped that my father, who did have a family to support, had become a district prosecutor. Who would dare to arrest the father-in-law of such a powerful local figure?

At different times, both my grandfather and I were hard on my father for his involvement in the communist machine. But now that I am older and know what it is like to have responsibility for a family, I can say that I understand why he made the choices that he did. And, although my grandfather would scoff, I was secretly very proud to have a father who was one of the few men in the town allowed to have a car with a driver, and all the other trappings of power. When you are young such things impress you. He would leave before I woke in the morning and return after I was asleep. To me he was an elusive figure of power and authority, although the seeds of doubt that my grandfather sowed in my mind left me uncomfortable about my father.

The system that my father had to work within was a mockery of justice; it must have been agony for him. State Security ordered the sentences and men like my father merely implemented them. Because he was the initiator of cases, my father was required by law to be present at the enforcement of the death penalty, along with the judge. I can only imagine what a devastating effect that must have had upon him, seeing men put to death for crimes that he had accused them of. When I was older I dared to reproach him about these cases. He looked at me with a dejected smile.

'Well,' he said eventually, 'you were very little. What could I do? Such were the times.'

That was how the system forced decent men to do indecent things and how the very fabric of Bulgarian society was destroyed so that now, over fifty years later, we are still reaping the whirlwind. But I was an ambitious boy and I was going to have to find a place for myself within this system.

CHAPTER TWO

A HAPPY CHILDHOOD BENEATH DARK CLOUDS

The midwife's words when she first saw me emerge from the womb set my mother off on a campaign to turn me into some sort of Renaissance genius. However well I did, she was determined to push me that extra few metres. I was a straight-A student, but when she arrived at my school as a German teacher she would stand over me during every break to ensure I was working as hard as possible and behaving immaculately. She pressed me into joining every club and course on offer in Stara Zagora, refusing to take any notice of my protests. She enrolled me for language courses, theatre courses, drama courses and literature courses. And then the notion struck her that I was destined to become a great musician, so she went out and bought me a violin.

For a year and a half I struggled through lessons with a Mr Voutchkov, who was first violinist with the Stara Zagora Opera and had two virtuoso sons of his own, before finally admitting to myself that I was a hopeless case when it came to the production of any musical sound whatsoever and deciding not to torture this kindly musician any longer with my dreadful mediocrity. The thought, however, of breaking this news to my mother, stamping on her bright aspirations, was more than I could bear. I continued taking the money for lessons twice a week but converted it, without the tiniest glimmer of shame, into hot dogs and sweets. I even convinced my father's official chauffeur, Zhelyo, to write my grades in the music report in his adult hand, garnished with fine words, claiming that I was near concert level standard. My acting courses paid off here and whenever I saw my mother returning home I would grab my violin and go into ecstasies of improvisation or some opus which I had learned off by heart simply for show.

But one day my proud mother met Mr Voutchkov in the street and discovered that the poor man had not seen me for nearly two years. I was waiting as usual to show off my prowess when she got home that day, but instead of being greeted with motherly tenderness and words of praise I was faced with a woman in a screaming rage. She snatched the instrument from my hands and reduced it to match-wood on my young head.

Even then she could not be dissuaded from believing in my genius and enrolled me in an equally tragic course to learn the accordion. When my brother was born, five years after me, the midwife did not make any predictions and he was allowed to develop at his own speed. My mother made it clear to me that I must always look after him, which I have done, eventually involving him in my businesses.

Despite the odd glitch, my mother's ambitions for me were a priceless gift for which I will forever be grateful. She kept me above the soup of mediocrity into which communism was plunging our country, and she taught me to acquire as many skills in life as possible, even those that I would never excel at.

One of the reasons I think I have sometimes succeeded where others have failed is my ability to get on with people.

A Happy Childhood beneath Dark Clouds

One of the best ways to do that is to share a common skill or interest. The more skills and interests you can develop, the greater your chances of being able to make contact with someone on a personal level. If I'm asked for advice by young people (I know they seldom want it), I tell them to learn as much as they can in the years before their hours are taken up with work and responsibility. Learn as many games and as many sports, as many languages and as many subjects as you possibly can. It may be that being able to play a game of chess or squash with someone will make the difference between winning a highly prized contract or job, and failing to do so; to be able to talk to someone in their own language about an author who is a native of their country can make the difference between being able to form a strong relationship or merely remaining on cordial terms.

There weren't many people living at that time who were being taught that to excel at as many things as possible is good. By murdering the country's finest citizens and draining the ambition from all those who remained apart from the politicians and criminals – who were all too often interchangeable and always interlinked – the communists managed to turn a great nation into a mediocre one, a situation that will take many generations to right itself. Because it was dominated by the Soviet Union for so many years, many people in the West are unaware that Bulgaria is a country in its own right. Many Westerners have been to Greece or Turkey for their holidays, but few realise that just to the north lies a country of even older history and pleasanter climes, home of the ancient Thracians as far back as 6000 BC. It's a land with one of the oldest cultures on earth; Orpheus, the greatest musician in history, was a Thracian.

Thracian princes and kings were described by Homer in the Iliad, half of them siding with the Greeks against the Trojans, others fighting as mercenaries for Troy. Later Thrace was conquered by the Romans. It was a Thracian nobleman, Spartacus, who very nearly managed to destroy the Roman Empire with his uprising of slaves and gladiators. The area was part of the Byzantine Empire until tribes of Slavs came down from the north at the end of the fourth century AD, and conquered everything down as far as the Greek islands. The Thracians and the Slavs lived peacefully together until the end of the seventh century when the proto-Bulgarians, former allies of Attila the Hun, arrived from the east and enriched the racial mix even further.

The Ottoman Turks invaded in 1396, and stayed for five hundred years, bringing with them the Muslim faith, and dragging local culture back several centuries. Throughout that half millennium the Bulgarians managed to preserve their religion, identity and traditions, dominating the local business and trade along with the Greeks, while the Turks preferred a lazier lifestyle.

The Russians eventually liberated the Bulgarians from the Turks, earning the nation's undying gratitude, a legacy of goodwill that allowed the Russians to return in 1944 unresisted. Although many Bulgarians hated the Soviet communist system, we always maintained our affection for the Russian people who we saw as our historical liberators; we believed that the Russians were suffering beneath the communist yoke even more terribly than we were.

The Red Army invaded in 1944 because Bulgaria was allied to the Germans. But the advisers to the king of Bulgaria (who was only four at the time), for historical reasons did not want to fight the Russians as the German army withdrew, and the communists were able to sweep through the country with barely a shot fired in anger. The most prosperous and developed country in south-east Europe, perfectly placed at the centre of the Balkans for trade all over the world, was consequently handed to the Soviets on a plate.

A Happy Childhood beneath Dark Clouds

The young King remained in the country until 1947, when the communists decided he might one day pose a threat. They organised a phoney referendum which resulted in a 99 per cent vote against maintaining the monarchy. The boy king was sent into exile in Egypt, one of the few countries willing to take in fleeing royal families at the time, accompanied by his mother who was the daughter of the last king of Italy. For a few years he went to school with a number of Arab princes. He then moved to Portugal where he was brought up with Juan Carlos, the exiled king of Spain. This is the same King who today as I write has been elected to power as the legitimate prime minister of Bulgaria – a unique achievement.

The geography of Bulgaria is as dramatic as its history, and the beautiful coastline alongside the Black Sea became the playground of the Soviet élite throughout the years of communist domination, walled off to normal citizens, its beauties jealously guarded, its luxuries carefully hidden.

So this was the country that I was born into and in my memory it was bathed in sunshine. In the summer the climate was mild and the landscape clothed in lime trees. In the winter the snow fell and we would be able to skate and sled on the Ayazmo, a mountain that lay beside the town. Despite the food shortages and the endless queues during the late 1940s, I felt secure and happy. I used to have a tin can that I would take to try to find milk each day, and there were coupons for everything, but I had never known any other way of living. For my parents it must have been very different. To have to queue for the basic necessities of life in a country which was famed for its cuisine, with dishes as good as anything to be found in any of the surrounding countries, must have been hard.

My paternal grandparents, who had been big landowners and millers until the arrival of the communists, had stayed in the countryside even after their lands were taken away. I would

Fighting it Out

still go to their village for visits, but more often I would go to my maternal grandfather's village of Opan, sometimes spending the whole summer there. Everyone knew everyone else in Opan, and most of them were related in some way. They called people from Stara Zagora 'market folk', because that was where the villagers went to do their marketing.

My Uncle Ilcho would take me out for long days on the riverbanks and meadows, teaching me to fish and shoot. We would go quail hunting in the autumn, rising at three or four in the morning with him travelling on his moped and me following on my bicycle, pedalling like a maniac to keep up. While waiting for the sun to rise we would rest and then move off across the stubble of the harvested fields. My uncle used me to run off ahead to frighten up the birds. After lunch we would fall into an exhausted sleep beneath a shady tree and when he tried to wake me I would pretend to still be asleep, putting off the hard twenty kilometre ride home for as long as possible. I passed my fishing skills on to the locals of Opan, showing them how to make rods, prepare bait and catch the carp trapped in the waters behind two new dams in the area.

The landscape around Opan was flat as a pancake, but there were a number of potholes, including a deep dark frightening well. My grandmother's stepfather, who was known as Grandad Lamby, had ended his life in this well, deliberately jumping to his death when he knew he was growing too old and sick to care for himself any more. He wrote a thank you note to everyone in the family and then jumped in. If you leant over the side you could just see the water glistening at the bottom like a tiny shiny coin.

Many of my relatives lived to great ages, often way past the century. My father-in-law had a saying: 'There is only one way to live to a great age, choose your parents well.' Both my parents are still alive and I have remarkably good health myself, despite the punishments that I've meted out to my body over the years.

A Happy Childhood beneath Dark Clouds

I remember riding a thresher in the threshing yard outside our village house, two or three of us being pulled along by a horse or a donkey. Then the winnower would blow the chaff from the grain, like a metaphor for life, separating the truth from the lies, the meanness from the dignity. I would carry lunch out into the fields for the reapers, the landscape baking in temperatures of forty degrees in the shade. One day a sudden storm darkened the sky like an early dusk, fearsome dark red forks of lightning stabbing out of the black clouds as the rain poured down. All the workers threw down their sickles and ran away from the trees and the cattle, because the skin of the cows was believed to attract the lightning. I lay, as I had been taught, face down on the flat ground with my feet pointing towards the thunder.

In Stara Zagora we played games with anything we could find, from marbles to cards. We made our own cards with pictures cut from cigarette boxes which we roamed the streets in search of, scouring the gutters. At the time disease was rife and every parent was frightened of polio, diphtheria and dysentery; they were horrified to hear that we were scavenging in the dirt for our playthings. Sometimes we would be beaten for the habit and one boy, Kuncho, who had the misfortune of having a doctor for a father, was constantly being jabbed with injections in the backside for one disease or another. Kuncho and I were part of a group of five who had been friends since the cradle. Our mothers had married at the same time and there was actually a picture of us all in a playpen together. Bonds like that stay with you for life and provide you with friends in adulthood who you can trust like brothers.

As well as playing football and dodge-ball, we also liked to fight with boys from other neighbourhoods, using sticks or slings or anything we could find. If we could draw the enemy's blood, so much the better. One thing that always united us and made us forget any differences we might have had was our war

Fighting it Out

against the occupants of Chadur Mogila, the gypsy quarter – and we fought them regularly The gypsies had been stopped from wandering in their caravans by the authorities, who wanted to be able to control them and force the children to attend school. They had been put into shanty towns and those who didn't make their living stealing worked as servants in the houses of anyone, like us, who had an official salary and could still afford to pay them.

Because my parents were so busy running around earning our daily bread (my mother taught German in school and was forced to tell the children that 'real' German literature only started in 1945), my grandmother, Rouska, did most of the work of raising me when I was home in Stara Zagora. I called her Baba and we did everything together like cooking and going to market. In the week before Easter we would paint eggs, knead sweet bread and bake the special butter biscuits that I was crazy about. Once my brother and I watched through the window while she was baking a batch of these biscuits. She locked them in a cupboard to cool and hid the key. We waited until she had left the room before recovering the key and releasing the cookies from their prison.

Baba and I read fairy tales to one another and played chess with the pieces drawn on cardboard squares as it was hard to find real ones. She would make small cups of Turkish coffee and we would sit together through the afternoons, putting the world to rights.

For all the troubles of my country, I knew that I was loved. Whatever heights a man reaches in life, if he has no milestones to show him the way back, he's not worth a penny. If you have a happy childhood you become a rock that nobody can destroy. The memories of childhood are islands on which the soul can rest. I have always stayed close to my roots. When I was small other boys who went away to camp during the holidays when I went to the village would mock me, but I didn't care. Whatever has happened to me since, I have never felt insecure because I have known that I could always go back to my village and grow watermelons, or sow grain and harvest it. I believe it's dangerous not to have somewhere you can go back to. Knowing that I had a home made me strong enough to go out into the world alone and brave enough to be willing to try and conquer the unknown.

But behind this idyllic childhood hung the dark ugly face of authority squeezing the lifeblood out of the country. Signs of cultural destruction were everywhere. It was fashionable to talk in bad Bulgarian, full of Russian words, and the grotesque bosses who strutted through everyone's lives, wore the same peaked caps as Stalin. There weren't that many Russians to be seen in the country; they were all hidden in the ministries in Sofia, working as 'advisers' to the ministers. But Bulgarians themselves suddenly became far more ardent communists than the invaders. Where just a few years before we had had virtually no communism in the country, now there were party members everywhere, informing, denouncing and inventing sins wherever they could, desperate to prove to the authorities that they were the most loyal of followers. They had slogans to fit every occasion. The worst sin was to be found 'ideologically untrustworthy'. It was a damning accusation, because once you had been accused of such a crime, you could never prove your innocence. There were no courts or police you could turn to. 'University graduates are fascists!' was another favourite slogan. There was even, 'People who sleep in pyjamas are fascists!'

It was like children calling one another names in the playground, while keen to show the teacher they are the best pupils. One of the new leaders in the town was a man called Chocho-olu, who was hailed as 'The Greatest Hero'. He lived two streets away from us and was a peasant in all the worst senses of the term. He was physically huge with enormous confidence born of arrogance and stupidity. The authorities claimed he was a great partisan, but we all knew he was a horse thief who had been hiding from the police when he came into contact with the underground Communist Party. All his tales, which were little more than strings of curses and terrible threats to the 'class enemy', were complete fabrications. In the coming years I was to meet many people like Chocho-olu and as long as they held any power or influence there was no hope for any of us.

When I was about eleven we were told that we had to vacate my grandfather's house. It stood next to a hospital, which he had designed and built, and had once owned. The authorities wanted to use the house as an extension of the hospital, so we were moved out into a small apartment in a block that my grandfather had also designed and built. It was the only new block in the town that was not a uniform communist grey. It had bright red balconies, a small sign perhaps that the authorities had not been able to stamp out completely the creativity and originality that had once dwelt in the Bulgarian soul. I had been incredibly lucky to have lived in the big house for as long as I did.

The first part of my childhood was effectively at an end. With other children of officials like my father, I was ready to be groomed for manhood among the élite of the country.

CHAPTER THREE

THE CHOSEN ONES

My friend Kuncho, the doctor's son, had two aunts who lived abroad, one in France and the other in America. When Khrushchev came to power in Russia and the atmosphere relaxed a little, one of his aunts sent Kuncho a big white Fiat car. Such a thing was unimaginable in a country where even most adults did not own a car. Furthermore, Kuncho had managed to acquire a driving licence at the age of sixteen.

We were in heaven as we toured back and forth between Stara Zagora and the Kazanluk baths, or out to Sluntchev Bryag (Sunny Beach), where they were laying the foundations for the mighty hotel complexes which would go up to accommodate the party élite and their guests in the coming decades. There were hardly any other cars on the road as we wove our way in and out of the horse-drawn carts from the cooperatives, feeling like young princes. Like most teenagers our main concern was partying, but our parties had to be secret. Almost everything fun was forbidden, which made it all the more exciting. Skintight trousers were the height of fashion and we would wear them at every opportunity. The guys from the Militsia would follow us around, waiting for an opportunity to slice our decadent clothing to shreds and teach us a lesson for daring to be different. They would do the same to any of the girls who dared to wear miniskirts.

Some of the boys had reel-to-reel tape recorders, which made them the greatest of heroes, invited to every party. These machines were so heavy it took three guys to carry them. Whenever someone's parents went away word would spread and a tape recorder would be taken to the house so that we could dance ourselves crazy to forbidden rock 'n' roll behind darkened windows and locked doors. The music was recorded from Western radio stations that the authorities made a fair attempt to block. We didn't care; even through all the static and distortion we knew what we were listening to. At one party, driven wild by the distant voice of Elvis Presley, we started jumping on the beds, which promptly collapsed beneath our weight. We knew that somewhere out there in the ether, beyond the border guards and barbed wire, was a world of glamour and excitement and we all wanted to know more.

On the evenings when there were no parties we would stroll along the Sturgaloto, a stretch of five hundred metres on the main street where everybody came out after six o'clock to see and be seen. We never made dates because we knew we would bump into each other there, wandering around like sheep, nibbling sunflower seeds and spitting the husks at other strollers, believing ourselves to be so cool.

Behind all this youthful swagger and posing, however, I was actually already a highly organised young man. My mother was seeing to that. Discipline at school was tough, but she didn't let the pressure ease during the holidays either. I don't remember a summer when I didn't read at least fifty books from the list provided by my form teacher. Even when I was brought down by sunstroke my mother kept me at it. On our first day of the school term she would stay up all night binding and covering my brother's and my books. Later she expected us to do it for ourselves. This perfectionism in everything has stayed with me right until this day. In my houses there is never a thing out of place; every knife and every fork has its home and I am not comfortable unless each one is put away. She instilled in me standards of personal grooming, right down to the cutting of fingernails, which have never left me. It's my belief that although we are born with 85 per cent of genetic make-up already decided, we can still develop the final 15 percent with discipline and hard work.

It's the genes of my ancestors, however, that have helped me most in life by providing me with an entrepreneurial spirit and a desire to seek the new, take risks and have no fear of the unknown. My great-grandfather, Mityo, was a wealthy man who bought some small ships and sailed them down the River Maritsa to trade with the Turkish Empire, through Greece and down to Cairo. When the river ended he continued out to sea and on his way back had to haul his sailing boats with ropes. He was an entrepreneur and a rebel whose horizons were greater than those of his fellow villagers. His tale, as told by my grandfather, seemed heroic to me. He also lived to be 115 years old. I felt sure I had a long and successful future ahead of me, if I could just find the right path to follow.

As I approached the age of fourteen I was told I'd been enrolled in a boarding school in Lovetch. I tried arguing, cajoling and finally crying in an attempt to dissuade my mother from sending me away from the family. She would hear none of it. This was part of her master plan for preparing me for the great destiny the midwife had predicted for me.

'It's the only language school in Bulgaria,' she explained patiently. 'Five years of training there will give you a considerable advantage in the future. No one can tell what will happen in the coming years, but they'll always need people who can speak more than one language.'

I have to admit she was right. I couldn't have been given a better grounding for success. Before the Russian invasion this German language school had been an American college. It stood on a hill, like a medieval fortress complete with fortified walls, as closed to the outside world as the Bastille. The communist powers viewed it as a hot house for future diplomatic, foreign service and security personnel. It was hard to get in and places were not allocated according to grades from entrance exams; it was a question of who you knew or who you were related to. The list of entrants was confirmed directly by the central committee of the Bulgarian Communist Party. My enrolment appeared to be accidental and caused a lot of arguments because my father was a leading member of the Bulgarian Agricultural People's Union – the closest thing there was to an official opposition party – before he became deputy chairman of the People's District Council. But my parents prevailed and I was allowed to stay.

Until then I had been under the impression that my father's position was unassailable, but I soon discovered this was not the case. He was a student of law in 1943, studying in Sofia, and among the brightest and the best. Because he had been expected to inherit all his father's lands, he was also a member of the Agricultural Union, which was by far the biggest party in the country. When the communists arrived it was the only other party that they allowed to continue, although they destroyed the existing leaders and promoted young men who could be more easily manipulated and intimidated, including my father. They put in puppets as bosses and pretended that the union was a separate party, an alternative to communism, just so that they could claim they were running a democracy. It was a complete sham, but my father was allowed to prosper within the union.

Firstly he became chief prosecutor for a province that

covered a fifth of the entire country. His job was to represent the state against criminals. He also had to act in a few political show trials as the prosecutor and demand death sentences for the accused. He had to attend the executions or he too would have been sent to one of the concentration camps they were building on swampy islets around the country. He would leave the house at midnight in order to watch men being shot for imaginary crimes he had proved they had committed.

In 1953, on the death of Stalin, my father became deputy governor of the Province. Khrushchev, who was himself no more than a peasant and illiterate until the age of twenty-five, had taken over in Russia and wanted more people from the Agricultural Union in power in Bulgaria. It was still a sham, but my father continued to prosper by it. As my father's son I had become part of the country's elite, which was why I was able to attend Lovetch, despite the fact that many party members would have considered our family 'ideologically unsound'.

A month before my fourteenth birthday my parents delivered me to the gates of Lovetch in my father's official car, leaving me on the wooden bridge to the school with a bunch of grapes in my hand and a lead weight in my stomach. Standing beneath those forbidding grey walls I felt as if the world was collapsing and my life had ended; in fact it had only just started. It was my first conscious experience of stepping into unknown territory.

The school was co-educational, with the girls and boys sleeping in separate buildings. We never needed to go outside the confines of the building. Everything was at our disposal: café, medical centre, theatre, gymnasium, park and a variety of sports grounds. The only thing we didn't have was an athletics track, so we trained at a local stadium. We were allowed to leave our dormitories between two and six in the afternoon on Sunday, and then only if we were not being punished for heinous crimes such as an untidy wardrobe or bed, or anything else the supervisors could think of. The habits of neatness and cleanliness that my mother had taught me were now drilled into me once and for all. From the moment I arrived I knew that in this mini-society I would have to be completely independent. Any influence anyone's parents had in the outside world was left completely behind; everyone had to rely on their own abilities and aptitudes.

We were together twenty-four hours a day, sleeping and waking, naked and fully dressed, in the bathroom or on the playing fields. We washed our own shirts and ironed our own trousers. Relationships and friendships were formed there that would last for the rest of our lives. We learnt to trust one another totally and still today I rely on old school friends should I find myself in trouble in Bulgaria or need someone I can trust to run a company for me. In the five or so years that we were together we became as close as blood relatives.

In each class there were five boys and fifteen girls and we were ruled with a rod of iron. We studied everything in German except mathematics, the Bulgarian language, painting and physical education. From eight in the morning until one in the afternoon we were with German teachers. In the afternoons we prepared for the next day with Bulgarian supervisors, who were proficient in German. Between seven and nine in the evenings we had extra-curricular activities such as photography, physics, literature, chemistry, politics, dancing, singing and theatre arts.

A system of eavesdroppers and informers, operating everywhere from the bathrooms to the games fields, ensured that we spoke German all the time. If you were caught speaking Bulgarian you received a black mark, which meant your grade was reduced. Three black marks and they docked your behaviour grade.

We were constantly told that we were the chosen ones, the

budding personnel of the party and future ministers of state. I was being indoctrinated twenty-four hours a day and I did not have my grandfather's balancing voice whispering in my ear. It was impossible not to be swept along with the crowd most of the time, but the seeds of doubt had been well sown in my subconscious and secretly I retained a scepticism that few of my classmates shared. Each Wednesday there was a political meeting, led by a supervisor or a more politically active student. The main purpose was to unmask any latent capitalism, and I knew from my own family's experience that if I had any doubts I should keep them to myself.

Despite the obvious political agenda of the school, it still managed to produce an extraordinary number of quality people – ministers, prime ministers, generals, professors, diplomats and writers – but very few of them managed to escape the system. The school didn't only concentrate on the development of the mind and all our sports teams were champions in the area. We grew up in an atmosphere of achievement and self-confidence. We were the elite and believed completely in our superiority. Even those pupils who went on to work for the party had slightly more European views of the political processes and about socialism than their more pro-Soviet colleagues.

Each evening we would go out jogging on the road to Troyan, from which we could see a concentration camp surrounded by barbed wire. We'd heard rumours about this place – of escaped prisoners and terrible hardships – but it was all third hand; none of us actually knew what was going on in that dreadful silent place. I knew this was the sort of camp my grandfather's friends would have been taken to, and I knew that if it wasn't for my father, my grandfather would be in there too, if he hadn't already been killed. The thought made me shiver and I preferred not to think about it. I had enough going on in my own life to occupy my young thoughts.

Fighting it Out

Although Stalin was dead, his malignant influence was felt everywhere in those years. Komsomol (the communist youth organisation) were watching every one all the time. We were constantly having orders barked at us: 'Get up!' 'Sit down!' 'Stand still!' Each morning, before entering the classrooms, two teachers would inspect our nails and collars for dirt, our chins for stubble, our trousers for creases and our hair for any signs of growth. We would march everywhere, singing marching songs at the tops of our voices, supervisors following us with whistles in their mouths, from six thirty in the morning until nine at night. It was like being in the army. They were training us in preparation for sending us out into the world to carry on with the cause. Although we were removed from the horrendous cruelties of the time, we were being prepared to play our part in the future of the grand Stalinist plan. There was little difference between the ways of the communists and the ways of the fascists, although I suspect the fascists may have been more intelligent and possibly therefore more humane, with some obvious exceptions.

Many of our teachers were misfits from the outside world. Our form teacher, who was also the PE teacher, was a man called Prisadaski who had the alarming habit of kicking your toes when he was talking to you, or grabbing one of your buttons and twisting it round until it finally came away in his fingers. He would then pop it into your pocket, continuing to talk as if nothing had happened. Whenever he was berating us for being idlers and for wasting the state's money, he would hold himself up as a shining example of a patriotic man, pointing to a scar on his forehead, which he told us he had received in the front line. One of the boys in our class, however, came from Prisadaski's native village.

'Comrade Prisadaski,' he said one day, standing up in front of the whole form, 'my father told me your scar is from a donkey that kicked you when you were a little boy.'

The Chosen Ones

The incensed teacher launched himself at the boy, beating him about the hands with the stick he used to wake us every morning, along with his referee's whistle.

Beneath the surface there was another command structure among the boys. Two gangs dominated the pupils out of sight of the authorities. One of these was led by myself and a friend called Brigo Asparuhov who, after the fall of the communists in 1990, became a general and chief of intelligence services. We inherited this gang from a boy who had been expelled shortly before his graduation, leaving us in charge while we were still relatively young. Brigo was in the eighth grade and I was in the ninth and together we ruled the dormitories. There were strict standards of conduct. No one was allowed to gossip, sneak or grovel to the authorities. Anyone caught committing these crimes would be punished on the spot in front of everyone. When a fight was needed between two boys we organised a boxing ring and gloves. We were the prosecutors and judges and developed our own understanding of justice, honesty and truth, right and wrong. We developed mechanisms for self-regulation and self-government, unwittingly preparing ourselves for the worlds of big business, diplomacy and politics.

In 1960 my mother arranged a three-month exchange visit for me to East Germany, to a town called Weimar. It was my first time out of Bulgaria and the memory I treasure most was a beautiful black shirt which I brought back to school with me to wear in the evenings, when we were allowed to change out of school uniform for a few hours. The first evening back I donned the shirt and felt like the most cosmopolitan and European of men. I strutted around for a quarter of an hour before a supervisor called me to one side.

'You will never put this shirt on again,' he instructed.

I took no notice, assuming the poor fellow was just jealous of my fashionable finery, and put the shirt on again the following evening. This time I was called over by the party

Fighting it Out

secretary for the school, a maths teacher who succeeded in putting me off that pleasant subject for life.

'You've been to Germany,' he muttered. 'That's all very well. But to bring back a black shirt like Mussolini!'

This apparently was my crime, to dress like a fascist. I was stunned, and even more so when I discovered my behaviour grade had been reduced simply because of the colour of my shirt. It was the first time I had personally felt the cold wind of official displeasure, but far worse was to come.

Back home in Stara Zagora the party comrades had decided to remove my father from his position as deputy chairman of the District People's Council. To be stripped of an office of such importance could only mean that my father had been branded an enemy of the party. It may have been that his crime was as trivial as mine, or it may have been that they had been watching him for years and looking for a way to bring about the downfall of a man who was not quite like the rest of them. All I knew was that as I was preparing to go to bed one evening, Lyuben, a schoolmate, brought a copy of the Bulgarian Communist Party newspaper into the dormitory and showed me an article about my father. I went to take it but he snatched it away and started reading it out loud in front of everyone. As I lay on the bed, listening, I felt a chill run through me. I knew this could be the end for our whole family. My father was accused of everything from political immaturity to distortion of the party line, of economic violations and every other sort of dishonesty. Many years later I would feel the force of the Western media against me, but at least I would have a free legal system to protect me. My father had no protection and the crimes of which he was accused could mean the death penalty. I was horribly alarmed but at the same time proud to have a father who had been brave enough to speak out against the system.

Later I discovered that for some time he had been voicing his opinions about how agriculture should be run in Bulgaria, so his fall was not as much of a shock to him as it was to me. But at the time, I felt terribly vulnerable; I was still only sixteen and completely helpless within a system which could do what it pleased with me. If they decided now to make me an outcast there was nothing I could do about it, no higher authority I could appeal to. All my mother's efforts to make me part of the country's élite, to give me the opportunity to make something of my life, would come to nothing.

Other boys started to giggle nastily as Lyuben continued reading, no doubt sensing that this would provide an opportunity for a shift of power in the dormitories. Perhaps they scented blood. I could feel the sands of potential treachery moving beneath my feet. I shouted at him to stop reading, but he continued. Furious and confused, I jumped from the bed and punched him hard. Lyuben rushed straight to the headmaster, knowing that I would no longer have any power to punish him for betraying our rules about sneaking. The headmaster, a cruel man and the perfect Stalinist, was still in his study, having stayed up to read the article himself. He listened to Lyuben's complaint against me and the next day I was expelled for fighting. It looked like the end of all my mother's hopes and dreams for my future.

I arrived back at the apartment in Stara Zagora in despair, my luggage all around me, to find my parents in an even worse state. If my father was taking his own fall from grace philosophically, he certainly wasn't taking mine in the same way. They were determined to do everything they could to save my career and stop me being dragged down with him, which meant pulling every string possible and calling in any favours or loyalties we might still be owed. In a communist country your very survival depends upon who you know and who owes you a favour. There's no other way to succeed; merit alone is certainly not enough and may even militate against you. But my father and my grandfather had made powerful friends along the way. Would any of them be willing to help, now that we had fallen from grace?

A family council of war was called that evening and, after much shouting and arguing and many tears, it was decided my parents would travel to Sofia, to seek help from Georgi Traikov, the most important and charismatic man amongst the agriculturists. Since my father had lost his official car, Anton, my godmother's husband, volunteered to drive them. My godmother, Radka, said she would also accompany them on this mission.

There was no time to lose and the party set out in the middle of the night, when all of us were at our most tired and emotional. My grandparents and I went to bed and tried to sleep, but it was impossible. I had been alarmed by the article and the headmaster's reaction to it; my parents' response had made me even more aware of how close to catastrophe we stood. A young man from a disgraced family stood no chance of ever making anything of his life in Bulgaria and had every chance of ending up in a prison camp. As I tossed and turned in my bed I imagined my father arriving in Sofia and waking his powerful friend, explaining the situation and them trying to work out a solution. I desperately wanted to believe that he would be able to save the situation for me. I wanted to get back to my studies and my friends as quickly as possible. Even then I knew that a good education might be my passport to a better life.

The next day an uncle rang from Sofia. He told my grandfather that he had just heard from my mother. I could see from my grandfather's face that it was bad news but I had no way of knowing how bad.

'What happened? What did Traikov say?'

'They never reached Sofia,' he replied, putting his arm around my shoulder. 'There was an accident on the road.'

'Accident?'

'They had to swerve to avoid an oncoming car. Irina rang

Traikov as soon as she regained consciousness.'

'Is she all right?'

'Yes, she's all right.' I knew from his tone that this was the best bit of the message. 'Your father and Radka are both dead. Anton's condition is critical.'

'They're dead?' I couldn't take the news in.

'She died instantly; he died in the emergency hospital in Sofia. They have instructed me to go and fetch the bodies.'

He left soon after. Two days later, after the obituaries about my father had appeared in the papers, detailing his illustrious career and glossing over his fall from grace, my grandfather made contact with me. He had the most extraordinary story to tell.

My father's body had been moved to the hospital morgue. A nurse, brushing past him to get some ice, accidentally knocked his hand off the trolley. Stopping to lift it back up she thought she detected a slight pulse and raised the alarm. The doctors rushed him out of the morgue, and by the time my grandfather arrived in Sofia my father was in the operating theatre, where they worked on his brain for ten hours. His whole forehead had been crushed by the impact and his cerebellum was gone. The doctors reported that it was hard to know what to do first, and impossible to predict how he would be once he woke up. The nurse who discovered the pulse has remained a friend of the family until today.

The first operation was followed by two more and he still did not wake up. For three months he lay unconscious as we all made our way to his bedside. Three months is a long time and in our hearts I think we never expected to be able to talk to him again, but then he woke. This, however, was not the father I remembered. This was not a strong, clever and experienced man of the world. This was someone coming into the world as if for the first time, like an innocent child, someone who had to be taught everything from how to walk onwards. He was also blind in one eye.

For a year and a half they kept him in hospital and re-taught him how to live. Compared to the horrors of that dark night on the road to Sofia, our family's political problems seemed to pale to insignificance, but it was an illusion. Our disgrace was still there in Stara Zagora, waiting for my father to return.

When he did eventually come home from hospital he found that his whole life had vanished. People who would previously have called him their friend and courted him for favours, now crossed over to the other side of the street when they saw him shuffling towards them. No one would even give him the time of day for fear they might be infected by whatever had brought him down. His mind seemed to have been dulled by the accident and the operations and he appeared not fully aware of what was happening around him, but my mother was acutely aware and could hardly bear the pain. She decided we would have to leave Stara Zagora and move to Sofia. When my mother decided that something was going to happen, it usually did.

While Sofia provided us with the anonymity that my mother had hoped for, our life was not easy. We were now living in poverty. My father had been retired as handicapped. His pension, even when added to my mother's modest salary, was hardly enough to feed two teenage sons. I wore my father's cast-off suits.

After a year of exile, whatever residual influence our family still had produced results and I was finally told that I could go back to school in Lovetch, to finish my education. When I saw the headmaster, Indjov, my old enemy, coming to meet me I felt sure it was some sort of trap and that he was going to send me straight back home. There was no trap; I was back in the school, but the evil of the man must have seeped into me because I vowed I would do anything to get even with him for the year of my life that he had stolen. I knew now that if I was to make anything of my life I could no longer rely on my family and their contacts. We had become outsiders and I was going to have to make my own way in the world. It was a daunting proposition, but I had all the confidence of youth. I should probably have been careful not to step out of line again, but that was not part of my make-up. I hated the headmaster so much for what he had done that I hatched a plan which, I can see now, was cruel if satisfying.

Indjov had two daughters and, I'm ashamed to say, I decided to use them as a way of getting back at him. They were very decent, pretty girls and Brigo and I set about chatting them up, flirting with them, holding their hands in the park and taking them to parties. We made it our mission to get these two poor girls to fall in love with us and didn't rest until we had succeeded. We then made a deal with one of the supervisors who was a good friend of ours. The deal was that he would catch us kissing the girls after lights out in one of the classrooms. The conscientious supervisor would then make a great fuss and report Brigo and me to the headmaster the following day.

'It's Atanas and Brigo, sir,' he duly reported. 'I caught them in an act of lechery with two of the girls.'

'Well done, Letunov,' Indjov boomed, rubbing his hands in anticipation of being able to get rid of two troublemakers once and for all. 'Bring the lover boys to my office, and the two girls as well.'

He had played into our hands. As the two loving couples were brought into his office the colour drained from the headmaster's face. His mouth opened and closed as if he was trying to communicate but no words came out. He waved us from the room and that was the last time we had any trouble with him.

As we grew older we grew bolder and would often flaunt the school rules, escaping at night through the garbage chute, where the fence was lower. It was on those late-night adventures that we tasted our first alcohol, smoked and mixed with the boys of the neighbouring town, disguising the smells with mouthfuls of garlic once we were safely back in the dormitories.

The adventure with the black shirt from Germany had whetted my appetite for fashionable clothes. In the West it was now the beginning of the 'Swinging Sixties' and young people were starting to express their individuality through their hair and clothes. We had few such opportunities, but we were always on the lookout for them.

When Radko, one of the boys from our class, managed to get hold of a plastic raincoat through his father, who worked for state intelligence, responsible for customs, we could hardly believe the beauty of this garment. We christened it Radunta and started a profitable business hiring it out to a long list of fellow students. Our popularity blossomed and Radunta was booked up months in advance. To step out into town in Radunta was a supreme experience and the girls would practically faint with delight at the sight of such high fashion, such slickness, such glamour.

By the time I was ready to leave Lovetch I knew that I wanted to study international commerce at the Institute of Economics since that might be my ticket to getting out of Bulgaria, but I also knew that before I could enrol there I would have to do my national service.

CHAPTER FOUR

LOVE FROM A COLD CLIMATE

All the self-discipline that had been instilled into me by my mother and then at Lovetch was cemented once and for all by the army. For the rest of my life I would be a man of fastidious personal neatness. In some ways it's a blessing, helping me to maintain serenity and order in my life, in others it's a curse, driving those who have lived with me to distraction. What can I do? It's the way I am.

In the army, with my head shaved nearly as clean as my chin, I was appointed a topographer in a village near Sofia. After the rigours of Lovetch, army life was a breeze. For a year I spent my nights on watch and my days studying reams of complicated material for the coordination of weapons. From logarithmic tables I had to add and subtract impossibly long figures and make mind-numbing calculations to reach some coordinate for shooting which, apparently, was essential for the accuracy of the fatherland's artillery. I became intimate with the hills near the Serbian border, patrolling from one elevation to the next, my trusty theodolite in hand. By the end of the year I'd mastered it and was able to do the sums with my

Fighting it Out

eyes closed. The army then decided to replace me with a jeep and a gyroscope. In my second year of army service I was a courier at army headquarters and I had to go to the Ministry of Defence every day to deliver the post. During this time there was a coup d'état and for two nights we were on full alert, although nobody thought to tell us what was going on.

In my spare time, of which there was plenty, I was able to read and prepare myself for the matriculation exams, as well as brushing up my languages. To study international trade I would need to take exams in a Western language, literature and geography. My studiousness paid off and, together with twenty-two other place winners, I proudly entered the Institute of Economics the autumn after leaving the army.

By the end of the first semester our numbers had ballooned to a hundred and none of our new colleagues had had to take any exams. All of them were the children of big party bosses and had managed to get there through string pulling, back doors and open windows. Having had my eyes opened to the corruption and deceitfulness of the state by my family, I was not greatly surprised by this turn of events. This new élite then arbitrarily declared that German was not a language of any worth and that the 'real' language was English, since most of them had arrived from the English language school, demonstrating the extraordinary flexibility of attitude which the communists are so good at. We who had got there by hard work and merit found ourselves the objects of disdain.

Not to be beaten I switched my attention to English and managed to pass the state exam with an 'Excellent'. I was not alone; some of my fellow students were studying five or six languages, including Arabic. We were preparing to take over the world.

While the theoretical education at the institute was broad, multifaceted and of a completely satisfactory standard, we were swamped by oceans of political nonsense and were given no practical knowledge at all. We had no idea what a contract looked like, or how to prepare a quote. Anyone who deviated from the correct political line would be marked out for life. One of my colleagues stood up in a political economy of socialism class one day and innocently asked how to equate the rotten nature of capitalism with the fact that our state import and export company and the state meat producers fed the American Sixth Fleet in the Mediterranean Sea. The authorities immediately put him down as a potential spy and enemy of the state. He had to go on explaining himself to a string of inquisitors for years to come. They eventually drove him to despair with their questioning and accusations.

In 1968 a group of us were sent to Prague for six weeks' work experience, in the midst of the city's political spring, directly before its tragic political summer. With my own eyes I witnessed the 'drunkenness of the people' as hope and euphoria spread at the prospect that communism could be put behind them and they would be able to move forward to socialism. We returned to Bulgaria in July and at the end of August the 'brotherhood of liberating armies' invaded Czechoslovakia and brutally demolished yet another attempt to break free of communism. The Soviet Union was sending a clear message to the world; it would brook no dissent in any form.

For that month however, we had been full of hope. We had returned home deeply infected by the contagious disease of freedom. Several of my more open-minded colleagues were chosen for membership of the Komsomol bureau, and I was promoted to Komsomol secretary. We started to hold pluralistic meetings and free discussions, confident that our time was close and so less cautious. But word must have been spreading about us behind our backs because we were forced to hold an extraordinary meeting at which we had to hand in our resignations. We had been categorised as revisionists,

Fighting it Out

opportunists and enemies of the state. It was obvious I was not going to be able to make a career for myself within the Komsomol.

Not every moment was taken up with serious political debating and study. We were young and as high-spirited as students in any other country. Next door to the Institute of Economics was the Higher Institute for the Performing Arts and we would spend many happy hours watching the girls go by.

'These girls will be entertaining us one day,' one of my fellow students shouted out one afternoon. The girls recoiled from us in loathing, but our self-confidence was such that we still had nothing but high expectations for our futures and plenty of short-term plans for debauchery. Despite numerous trips to the nearby Vitosha Mountain and long crazy parties in chalets, I continued to receive top marks. Years later, when I applied to the Helsinki School of Economics and Business Administration for an acknowledgement of my Bulgarian diploma, Professor Honko, a renowned economist, called me in.

'Young man,' he said, 'I will acknowledge your Bulgarian diploma only due to the fact that you were a top student. But I must tell you that half of what you studied is utter rubbish!'

What he was referring to, of course, were the many political subjects in the curriculum, starting with the history of the Bulgarian Communist Party, which was taught to us by Comrade Tsokovitch, a Serbian from Yugoslavia whose main occupation was chasing women. Professor Honko explained that while Marx may have come up with a number of truths in his economic analysis in Das Kapital, the idea of studying the political economy of socialism was ridiculous. The theories were as hopeless as the practice.

At the time Comrade Tsokovitch had seemed deeply impressive. To us students, living in our isolated nation, Yugoslavia seemed as distant and glamorous as Switzerland. I had met some of the Yugoslavian representatives in Sofia by chance. They seemed exceptionally nice people with unearthly riches and opportunities, which gives an idea of just how impoverished we were in both departments. I was desperate to get my hands on some of their cosmopolitan chic. Having managed to accumulate my first capital from a holiday job (the princely sum of fifteen dollars, if I recall correctly), I asked one of the Yugoslavians, a man called Tomé, to buy me a plastic jacket on his next trip home. I was desperate to wear something other than my father's worn and shapeless cast-off suits.

'I'll pay for it,' I assured him.

A few weeks later he brought me the jacket and I proudly held out the ten dollars I knew it had cost. He looked me up and down.

'Put your money away you old down and out!' He grinned. Five years after setting eyes on the blessed Radunta at high school, I now had a plastic jacket of my own. Progress was slow.

The holiday job I had found was to prove, eventually, to be my passport out of Bulgaria. My girlfriend, whose parents had serious political connections (her mother was teaching German to future spies in the Secret Service school), had managed to get employment as a part-time interpreter for the foreign department of the Central Committee. Her work involved meeting, accompanying and seeing off any foreigners who visited Bulgaria by invitation of the party and state leadership. In the summer that usually meant taking them to Evksinograd, the holiday resort on the Black Sea which was reserved for Bulgarian ministers, party leaders and general secretaries of the comrades' parties and their families. How we envied her ticket to enter this forbidden paradise.

One beautiful September day I received a telephone call from my girlfriend. She had a problem and asked if I would be able to take over her duties for two weeks. 'I'm due to accompany a delegation from East Germany,' she told me. 'I've

Fighting it Out

taken the liberty of recommending you to my head of department who is responsible for the guests of the Central Committee. I hope you don't mind.'

Mind? I didn't mind in the least. In fact, from that moment I was on tenterhooks waiting for the man to call me. Like everyone else I had heard stories of the wonders to be had in places like Evksinograd, where the great and powerful were rewarded for their effort and loyalty with unbelievable luxury; I longed to be able to experience it for myself. I could also see that this would be the perfect opportunity to mix with interesting and important people and to learn something of the outside world and how it worked.

I didn't have to wait long. The call came the following day and I was given the job. If I made a good impression I knew I would be invited back. That was how the system worked. Now I would get to spend my summers at the coastal town of Varna and at the resorts around it, ushered inside through the high fences, past the guards and on, to experience the wonders of life at the top.

The reality was every bit as exciting as the myth. The stories had not been exaggerations; this was indeed paradise. There were powdery sandy beaches stretching for tens of kilometres, and beautiful parks with spectacular mountains towering behind. The hotels that the Soviets had built contained what to me then seemed unbelievable luxuries. There was the best food and drink on earth, mountains of it with no queues in sight. It was a million miles from the grey world of shortages and food coupons which most of us were used to in our normal lives.

Apart from the beauty and luxury of the place, it also had the highest concentration of powerful people in the world. Anyone who was anyone in the Eastern Bloc, from the Soviet Politburo down, could be within those hotel compounds. There was no Western equivalent to this place; nowhere you would find the leaders of France, England and America holidaying and talking together on a regular basis, along with their ministers, generals and secret policemen. Nor was it limited to grandees from communist countries; there were also people from countries like Italy, France and America. I was immediately struck by their intelligence and the breadth of their understanding of the world, compared to the sycophants, bullies and puppets I was used to seeing in the lower echelons of local politics.

At the other extreme there were also visitors from countries like Mongolia and Kazakhstan who behaved little better than animals and conducted political discussions that made me cringe with embarrassment at their naïvety. I could also see great differences between the communists from Eastern and Western Europe, both in the standards of their behaviour and in their understanding of life and communist ideology. The Eastern Europeans were distinguished by their extraordinary sectarianism and stupidity, while the Westerners, although still communists, had a considerably more humane attitude towards others and much more progressive views.

I also got to accompany visitors from German-speaking countries on tours around Bulgaria. Often they were there to give lectures and talks in provincial towns and I was able to speak with them during most of their waking hours. Apart from the money and the physical perks of being able to stay in the same hotels and eat in the same restaurants, I was able to learn about the world outside Bulgaria's borders from these elite guests. I was socialising with heads of state and people of international renown. To begin with it felt strange to be face to face with men who were viewed by millions as political icons and saints, and usually only seen from a distance reviewing huge military parades. I had read about these leaders in the newspapers all my life and now not only was I required to have breakfast, lunch and dinner with them, I would also play volleyball on the beach with them, all of us in swimming

Fighting it Out

costumes and behaving like equals.

I quickly got to know and understand the workings of the political bureaux and central committees of the socialist countries. I was swept around Bulgaria in limousines with them, their families and friends, watching as they were given everything they asked for. They opened my eyes to the way things were, reminding me of the things I had heard at my grandfather's knee about the trappings of power and the realities of the system which purported to bring equality to all.

The sheer weight of bureaucracy in the Soviet system was beyond belief. The central committee of the party trusted no one, and so doubled up on every job. Where there was a ministry of defence in a country, there would also be a department of defence, which was made up of people from the central committee and held the real power. The people who came to the resorts were invited by officials of the department of foreign relations, who were infinitely more powerful than any foreign minister, and it was the department of foreign relations that hired people like my girlfriend and me.

Such a lucky break could not come without a price, and back at the institute there was jealous talk about my good fortune. Komsomol members and the party leaders at my faculty were furious that my interpreting jobs meant I did not have to work on farms or in factories and other state enterprises during the summer holidays like everybody else. The idea of me sitting on beaches or in luxury hotel bars while they sweated and toiled in the fields or on noisy assembly lines was more than these people could bear. Fortunately for me I had a teacher of currency and finance who managed to explain to the members that translating at governmental level was also a job and not simply an escape from responsibility.

Now that I was moving in such exalted company I had to be even more wary of how I behaved. A casual remark which might have gone unnoticed from a mere student was likely to be jumped upon if it came from someone moving in such high circles. It would have been easy to give those who resented me the ammunition they needed to remove me from my new privileged existence. Once, when escorting an East German professor of economics on a speaking tour, I relaxed enough to tell him a joke about the Russians. I thought nothing more about it until my employer called me in some weeks later and showed me a letter which the professor had written to the Central Committee once he got home, suggesting that I was not trustworthy because I made jokes about the Russians. Luckily for me my employer was understanding, but it taught me just how dangerous it was to relax completely, because you never knew what the person you were talking to was actually thinking, or where their sympathies lay.

Some of the guests who filled the Varna governmental resorts were Latin Americans. They were all introduced with false names and I was not officially allowed to spend time around them, but my English was good enough to be able to exchange a few words. I discovered they were all big names from the revolutionary communist guardia. This was the height of the Cold War, a time when the East and the West were totally opposed and both doing everything they could to win the hearts and minds of people in Third World countries.

I was always very aware that the ultimate intention of the Soviet system was to conquer the world and I was constantly afraid that they would go as far as starting a nuclear war simply because of their mediocrity and the slave mentality that made them willing to obey orders, however stupid those orders might be.

At a grand feast in honour of the invasion of Czechoslovakia, Western visitors were horrified by the ignorance they heard displayed. It was like witnessing the feasting of the barbarians after the fall of Rome. The booze flowed like a river and the singing, kissing, embracing and

Fighting it Out

rejoicing at the victory of 'our armies' went on long into the drunken night. When the news of the invasion first came in, many of the Westerners packed and left immediately in protest. Having been in Prague just a few months before I understood their views and felt a terrible sadness at the lost opportunities this crushing of the Prague spring meant. It seemed none of us were destined to crawl out of the Dark Ages for a little while yet.

Before I became an interpreter I had never met any of these important people, knowing them only by their propaganda like everyone else. So, to begin with, I saw them as almost godly in their power and wisdom. As time passed I realised how limited and vain most of them were, and there were many times when I wanted to die of shame. They understood little or nothing of the problems they discussed with their colleagues from abroad and sometimes spouted utter nonsense. To save my own blushes I tried to take the discussions into my own hands whenever possible. I would leave the big boss talking nonsense and develop the topic in the way I thought best. I translated only the most crucial things literally. The foreign guests would nod contentedly, gratified at how clever our leaders were.

I realised as I met many of the most important men of the time that Bulgaria was in an age of spiritual darkness. People who lacked a single original or humane thought had been installed to manage the country because they showed the greatest blind loyalty to communism and were the easiest for the party to control. It was madness. Not only were they entirely unaware of their ignorance, but they showed no signs of wanting to educate themselves, believing they were already at the summit of human achievement. They had the brains of newborn puppies, talking in clichés and praising their superiors whatever they did. If Khrushchev wore a cloth cap, they would all wear cloth caps. If Khrushchev wore a trilby they would do the same. If you spoke to one of them it was the same as speaking to all the rest; you could predict exactly what they would say. Anyone who showed any originality or humanity was immediately banished or disappeared.

This was the greatest education I could have asked for at such a young age. I was at the top without being part of it. At the very summit of the Bulgarian pile was Todor Zhivkov, the general secretary of the Bulgarian Communist Party. Everything in the state sprang from him. Having interpreted for him in those early years, I later met him again at a ski resort in the Rilla Mountains when I was a Western businessman, and he gave me a watch made in his home town, bearing his signature on the back. I passed it on to my father, telling him to wear it with the signature facing up to impress his neighbours.

My interpreting skills were used more often at political discussions than at commercial ones, sometimes even at meetings of the Warsaw Pact. My understanding of how the communist world worked moved forward in leaps and bounds and I was soon able to hold interesting conversations in my own right, as if I was already a man of the world.

At the time the general belief was that communism would last for ever because it looked after people from the cradle to the grave. No chink could ever be allowed to appear or the entire system would immediately have collapsed. In order to manipulate people the authorities had to brainwash them, which meant allowing no external information to reach them. Every scrap of information, news and opinion emanated from one source and supported one doctrine. Every citizen was totally at the mercy of the regime, as unprotected as if they were already in a concentration camp, which in a way they were.

The leaders were producing people like battery chickens, or robots, all thinking and speaking in the same way, everything governed by political education. We had become a race of zombies, and once a person has become a zombie it's almost impossible to bring him or her back to life. Communism is like ideological radiation; it takes years for its destructive powers to disappear. The results are easy to see to this day: our people lack the simple criteria of good and bad, right or wrong. Every villain in Bulgaria can be turned into a martyr and the few decent people can be reduced to the dregs of society.

The sins of the Bulgarian communists are well known. Less well known are the sins of the Bulgarian Orthodox Church, which allowed this spiritual devastation to happen. For centuries the Church has failed to do its job, its leaders preferring to hide away in monasteries and churches rather than speaking out and attempting to provide the people with moral backbone. It has always linked itself to those in power rather than facing the problems of ordinary people. The priests should have been opening our eyes to the lies and hypocrisy that we were living under and the crooks and charlatans who were leading us, but they stayed silent. In countries like Poland, Czechoslovakia and Hungary the Catholic Church never deserted its people. It never became part of the governing system, always striving to be close to the people, to preach and to bring its lost sheep back onto the right path. As a result the Catholic peoples have found their way more quickly since the fall of communism.

By giving me a job as an interpreter, the authorities had provided me with the greatest of gifts: they had removed any illusions I had left that I wasn't living under a system of lies. They opened my eyes and once that has happened you can no longer be a victim of the propaganda. I could no longer be a slave because I had seen the truth of my servitude. But in Bulgaria at that time there was no alternative to servitude apart from joining the system. There was no resistance organisation or opposition party I could have joined. Everyone was equally enslaved. I knew the people in power and I knew the children who would be stepping into their shoes. Nothing was going to remove them from power in the foreseeable future. I needed a miracle to save me.

When the miracle arrived at first I did not recognise it. It came in the form of Georgi Andreev, a friend of my father and one of the few clever people left in the Agricultural Union. He came to look for me on the beach one day.

'I urgently need an interpreter,' he told me. 'I'm going to meet the Finnish minister for foreign affairs. His plane lands in three hours' time.'

'Don't you have your own interpreter?'

'Yes, Amalia. She's otherwise engaged. Can you do it?'

'Of course.' My family had known Andreev a long time; I would not have wanted to let him down. I quickly changed from my swimming costume into a suit and tie.

His limousine took me out to Bourgas airport to meet an ordinary tourist flight from Helsinki. I was surprised. I was used to megalomaniac officials chartering private planes and insisting on a great deal of fuss wherever they went. The authorities let us out onto the runway, with all our pomposity and imagined superiority, to meet the gentlest, most modest of families as they came down the steps of the plane among the other passengers.

Dr Karjalainen, a completely normal and decent man, was one of the two most powerful people in Finland for around thirty years. Sometimes he was prime minister, sometimes he held other ministerial posts. He was a member of the Centre Party, which had no leftist leanings at all, but the Russians were extremely anxious to cultivate good relations with the powers in Finland. They had an idea that if they could peacefully persuade Finland to become communist, then it would act as a model for other European countries to follow. They knew that Dr Karjalainen was on good terms with the

Fighting it Out

Agricultural Union in Bulgaria and they wanted to exploit that relationship to improve their links with Helsinki.

That year he was minister of foreign affairs and he was accompanied by his quiet sixteen-year-old daughter and her two brothers. As we made our way across the tarmac to the limousine I had no idea I was escorting my future wife and father-in-law.

Her name was Kukka-Maaria. Kukka means flower. Although I had heard that Scandinavian girls could be a lot of fun, to me she was just a charming child. With the rest of them I spoke German, but on the rare occasions I spoke to her it was in English. In an attempt to entertain her while her father was in meetings, I took a boat to show her around the beach. For the whole trip she didn't utter a single word. She seemed the most timid of creatures; I had no idea what might be going on inside her head. After a few days Amalia, the official interpreter, arrived, and my services were no longer required. I left without thinking any more about it. It had been just one more interesting meeting with people from Western Europe.

I must have made some sort of impression on Kukka-Maaria because she wrote to me once she was back in Finland. We exchanged a few letters and the following summer she returned to Bulgaria with a friend, to a resort north of Varna. This time it was a private visit. We saw each other, went out together several times and started a sort of affair. She was a little hurt that my friends and I appeared to neglect her most of the time, but to us she still seemed like a child. When she got back home to Helsinki she sent me an angry letter, telling me how terrible I was to have seen so little of her when she had come all that way to see me. That winter we exchanged more letters and now they were not so innocent. Kukka-Maaria was growing up and our feelings for one another were becoming more serious.

Love from a Cold Climate

I decided I wanted to travel to Finland to see her and to visit a Western country. By then it was 1970. I was twenty-six years old but I still hadn't graduated from the institute. I had made some important connections through my work and I knew just who to approach in order to obtain permission to travel. I was friends with the son of the Bulgarian ambassador to Finland – a member of the central committee I had met at the resort – and this provided me with another reason for making the trip and gave me somewhere to stay, so I didn't have to worry about how to afford hotel accommodation. Eventually I was given permission to travel and, after some mighty quarrels with my family, I managed to borrow some money from my father and a fur coat from my cousin's son. I then boarded a train for Helsinki, travelling via Moscow, heading into the middle of the notorious northern European winter.

I had been to the West only once before, when I had travelled to Vienna with a group of provincial Communist Party secretaries on an exchange trip. Just driving around the centre of the city in the official cars it was obvious to me how different the West was. I had seen shops filled with goods I had no money to buy and people on the streets enjoying a lifestyle I could only dream of. Now, as I sat huddled in my borrowed fur coat, watching the vast icy expanses of Russia going by outside the train windows, I prepared to sample the pleasures of the West for myself, my heart thumping with excitement and expectation.

CHAPTER FIVE

ENTERING A DIFFERENT WORLD

I knew nothing about Finland. For me it was a leap into the dark. I might have visited Vienna and seen the surface of life in the West, but I had still been part of an Eastern European delegation. I had not actually been thrown into a foreign culture on my own.

Finland was not how I had imagined. The country was cold and grey, the nights seemingly endless and the ground covered in snow. The contrast with Bulgaria was total, but that added to the excitement for a young adventurer. The Karjalainen family welcomed me with warmth and simplicity; there were no ostentatious shows of hospitality, no drunken feasts or lavish gifts, just politeness and kindness. Kukka-Maaria and I knew immediately that we wanted to be together and so, like the young fools we were, we decided to announce our engagement; never mind that we were both still studying and lived in different countries, one of which was a communist state. Her parents gave their blessing and never for one moment let me see the worries that they must have had at their daughter attaching herself to such an exotic creature as a Bulgarian communist. It was an immense act of faith on all our parts.

Fighting it Out

Dr Karjalainen was prime minister of Finland three times in all. He was minister for foreign affairs for sixteen years as well as minister for trade and industry, deputy manager of the National Bank and co-chairman of the Finnish-Soviet Upper Governmental Committee for Economic Relationships. In a country with fifteen political parties President Kekkonen and he governed for thirty years in democratic and pluralistic conditions, bringing Finland immense security and prosperity despite all the political difficulties of its past.

Joining such a well-connected family in the Eastern Bloc would have meant being showered with gold, immediately being given the key to the house and the car and every privilege available. I soon realised that in Western Europe there was a very different approach to bringing up young people in such families: to make them work just like everyone else, maybe even a little harder than everyone else. In Bulgaria the powerful were so well protected and looked after by the security service, they never had to worry about their material needs. In Finland the prime minister's family were like anyone else. There were no special estates that they could be given to live on, no government villas or other privileges. My future father-in-law's telephone number and address were listed in the local directory and when someone rang the doorbell he would answer it himself and speak to whoever was there. Such a concept was impossible to imagine under communist rule.

After I had overcome my initial shock, Dr Karjalainen's modesty impressed me enormously, such a dramatic contrast to the strutting arrogance and ignorance of the Eastern leaders I had met. He would have considered it appalling taste to show off his position, his health or his wealth. To have pulled any strings to help me would have been political suicide, and it would never have occurred to him to do so. He was among the cleverest and most gifted people I have ever known, with a wide range of interests. The first year he was prime minister his three sons worked on construction sites, carrying buckets of cement like all the rest, and Kukka Maaria worked as a shop assistant. All his sons went on to graduate with top marks, two of them becoming doctors and the other an architect. Kukka-Maaria completed her Ph.D. and has so far written three books.

The Karjalainens reminded me of a story my grandfather had told me as a child about his own education in Karlsruhe in Germany.

'I shared a room and all the misery of poverty with a nice German boy,' he had said. 'For five years we shared everything, down to the last penny. Every holiday my friend would invite me to come with him to his parents' place, but I refused because I was so anxious to get back to see my wife and children, and I didn't want to be any trouble to his family. I didn't want them to have to worry about feeding another mouth.

'When we finally graduated as architects, however, he invited me again and I accepted, thinking that it might be my last chance to spend time with my friend. We travelled third class on the train to Berlin and were met at the station by a huge limousine with a uniformed chauffeur who drove us to a mansion overlooking the Wannsee. We were greeted by an army of servants who took our bags and tended to our every need. That evening I discovered that my friend's father was an entrepreneur. He built immense housing estates and employed dozens of architects.

'I said to the father, "at least your son will have a good job now. I have to go back to Bulgaria and start from scratch". He shook his head and told me his son would not work for the family company but for a competitor, where he would learn to fight and win.'

At the time it had seemed like something of a fairy tale, but now I could see that was how things worked in the capitalist economies, and I could see how healthy it was.

Fighting it Out

It must have been a shock to my future parents-in-law to discover that their daughter wanted to marry a Bulgarian interpreter they knew nothing about, a man who travelled on a communist passport. But they never made me feel that they were worried or disappointed in any way. They treated me as an adult and an equal. Perhaps, in their wisdom, they thought that after I had returned home to graduate I would never be allowed to leave Bulgaria again and that would be the last they would see of me. They certainly didn't offer to help me to stay in Finland, but then that would not have been their style.

At the end of my holiday, I returned to Bulgaria and the institute. A few months later my grandfather bought me my first new suit ever for my graduation ceremony. I felt very proud of myself, but I had no idea how I was going to get back to Finland and to my fiancée. I knew there was no way she could be expected to give up the rest of her schooling and come down to Bulgaria; it had to be me who made the first move if we were to be together. But how to go about gaining permission, that was the question. The alternative was to take a job within the Bulgarian system and hope she would be able to join me later. That didn't seem an attractive proposition.

I decided I had nothing to lose and everything to gain by getting sent to Helsinki. Like a gambler heaping all his chips onto one spin of the wheel, I went round every contact and connection I had ever made at school, at university or through interpreting, telling them I wanted to be sent to Finland, begging to be given any sort of job. But everyone I spoke to about the subject either laughed or shook their head in hopeless pity. I was only twenty-six years old, they pointed out, and had never had a permanent job, so what could I offer in the way of experience to an employer? On the other hand, I answered back, I had no access to any secret documents and I was no threat to national security, so why should I not be able to find a foreign posting of some sort?

Entering a Different World

I got nowhere. In the end, like everyone else in my beleaguered country, I had to resort to string pulling. Georgi Andreev agreed to go to Todor Zhivkov, the most powerful man in the country, and ask him to allow me to go to Finland to get married. Quite rightly, Zhivkov told him to stop bothering him with such nonsense, that it should be sorted out by someone further down the hierarchy. That did the trick. If Zhivkov said it should be dealt with by someone else, there would be no shortage of people eager to do the bidding of such a great man.

My persistence had paid off. Using Zhivkov's name I went back to my contacts and started again. In truth they had probably grown so tired of hearing from me that they decided to do anything to shut me up. I was given a lowly post as an assistant attaché at the embassy in Helsinki. My job was to compile economic analyses and reports on the development of Finland. It was a non-existent position according to any ministerial job descriptions, which had been invented simply to give me something to do. It was a perfect example of how string pulling worked and how rotten the whole system was. Who cared? It was working to my advantage at last although everyone I came into contact with immediately suspected that I had planned the whole thing just to get out of Bulgaria.

How could I possibly have dreamed up such an elaborate plan? How could I, a humble interpreter, have deliberately got myself introduced to Dr Karjalainen and made his daughter fall in love with me? It was ridiculous but from the day I arrived at the embassy in Helsinki I could feel myself being followed, day and night by suspicious envious eyes.

My first lodgings in the city that was to become my home for many years, were the size of a wardrobe. Inside my tiny room there was no furniture whatsoever, not even a bed. I was given a mattress on the floor and two stools, but no money. I had a symbolic salary, but that was all it was, symbolic, because an assistant attaché's allowances were not included since the position didn't officially exist. But I was young and I saw none of this as an obstacle to making my way in this new and strange country. My friend, the Bulgarian ambassador's son, was studying at the university and we would eat together in the university canteen.

Through my work I got to meet Finnish and other diplomats, gradually penetrating deeper into diplomatic society, but returning each night to my mattress on the floor between two stools. All around me were the trappings of comfortable life, but I had no way of getting any of them for myself. Like many young men, I had a particular eye for good cars. The best car in the embassy was a Mercedes 330D which was owned by the ambassador's driver. He was a half-literate peasant, but when he was behind the wheel of that car he looked as proud as a king. He had two children at school and his wife didn't work and I just couldn't see how he had been able to afford such a beautiful machine on a driver's salary.

'How do you do it?' I asked when we were waiting together one day for the ambassador. 'Your salary can hardly pay for food in this city, yet you've managed to buy a Mercedes.'

'Well,' he slapped me on the back, happy to be able to help a young man out with some worldly advice, 'my wife found a small shop round the corner selling canned food. Very tasty, you know, and very cheap. We've been eating it for years now. It has cats on the label.'

I was stunned into silence. He had been feeding his family on cat food for four years in order to be able to drive a Mercedes! That was a price I didn't think was worth paying.

He was replaced soon afterwards by another driver, a great fellow who couldn't speak any foreign languages but had no difficulty getting round shops using gestures and facial expressions to show what he wanted. One day I heard him talking to the housekeeper at the embassy.

'Hey, Ivan, tell me how to say "condom" in Finnish, so I

Entering a Different World

don't have to point at my thing in the pharmacy.'

Living in a foreign country can be difficult in a thousand little ways. The change between one culture and another, one language and another is enormous and cannot be imagined by anyone who has never done it. Moving from the south to the north I had to accustom myself to a completely different way of doing things, different ways of behaving, eating different meals at different times of the day. I had to change my attitudes as well as my habits. Finland at that time was a very closed society. Few Finns spoke foreign languages and they were deeply suspicious of outsiders, perhaps because of their vulnerable border with the Soviet Union. For many years Finland had been isolated from the rest of the world, firstly by the sea, secondly by its border with Russia and thirdly by its language. The Finns have never seen anything good in their neighbours, especially the Slavs in the east; they have been fighting wars on that front for centuries. Finland and Sweden were one country for seven hundred years, with Finland the subordinate. During wartime the Swedes provided the officers and the cavalry while the Finns provided the infantry. Historically, the big money was with Swedish-speaking families and Stockholm dominated, although Helsinki is now growing.

Because of their history the Finns are a cautious nation, slow to open up, and it is extremely difficult for a foreigner to make friends, but if you win the trust of a Finn it will last a long time. This was an enormous culture shock for me; coming from the south where you embrace the person next to you while you drink together and declare him to be your greatest friend. I found Finnish reserve quite shocking, seeing nothing but closed, shy people who wanted to make no contact. A Finn, for example, will never speak a word of a foreign language until he's convinced he's fluent in it, whereas a Bulgarian will wade in, thinking he's communicating beautifully, when he has no more than a few words.

Fighting it Out

Finns are the greatest of patriots and taught me exactly what the word meant. They are so patriotic they are sincerely convinced of their duty to pay taxes. They do not, like most other peoples, see taxation as robbery on behalf of the state but as something it is a citizen's duty to pay. It doesn't even occur to them to work out ways of evading tax because they know that by paying taxes they create a wealthy state that can protect them and provide education and pensions. By comparison the societies of Russia and Bulgaria seemed primitive.

In 1939 and 1940 Finland stood alone against the might of Soviet Russia. Although they were only four million people they still managed to resist the Soviet army and held on to their entire border of over a thousand kilometres.

When peace was signed with Russia in 1940 the Finnish gave up their old border, which was very close to Leningrad, and moved it nearly fifty kilometres north to Murmansk. After the Germans' iron siege of Leningrad in 1941, the only possible way for supplies to reach the town was across the Ladoga Lake. At the same time a secret understanding was reached with the Soviets stating that Finland would not cross the old border in exchange for the Soviets being obliged not to destroy Finland after the war. In 1945, after the capitulation of Germany, the Russians took just one small peninsula, called Porkkala, and an island from Finland, but otherwise behaved very correctly and no real occupation of the country was attempted. There were Russian soldiers and officers present only at the military bases that Khrushchev had given back to the Finns in 1956, under great pressure from Kekkonen and my future father-in-law and a long time before the agreed deadline.

Having been allied with Nazi Germany, Finland had to pay huge reparations after the war in gold and Western currencies corresponding to the gross national income. It was the only country that paid the reparations to the last penny. This had a positive influence on the country because until then it had been mainly undeveloped forest and badly kept agricultural land, but the reparations forced them to take enormous credit from abroad in order to develop their industry and pay their debts.

Considering it still only has a population of five million, Finland now has enviable economic power. It became wealthy by way of clever politics, relationships with other countries, and by trading with the massive Soviet Union. My future father-in-law was the founder and architect of this strategy.

Immediately after the war Finland was pushed out of Western markets because it was a former ally of Germany. The ascendance started in around 1954, when Kekkonen became prime minister and my future father-in-law was his cabinet chief. Very humbly and quietly, they laid down the economic basis that later put Finland into the fast lane, winning markets in the Soviet Union, Western Europe and the United States. During the early eighties, when the USSR was in its prime, the Soviet Union comprised around 24 per cent of Finland's foreign trade. Although Germany and France were bigger trading partners with Russia, it was the Finnish who were considerably ahead in per capita trade turnover.

Unlike many other countries that wasted their post-war profits on cars and recreational facilities, the Finns reinvested all their money wisely in the modernisation of their enterprises. It was as if they felt that the good times would not last forever and they were right, because after the fall of communism in the USSR, trade between the two countries dropped to zero. Finland, however, came safely out of the crisis and has at its disposal today super-modern, progressive and exceptionally competitive industry. They are now one of the richest free-market welfare states in the world.

Many books have been written, describing how the Soviet Union oppressed, manipulated and controlled Finland. I did not see that happening. The Russians were extremely aggressive, especially at the time of crisis during the early

Fighting it Out

1980s when they were not keeping up in the arms race and were suffering from an economic crash. But at all times I saw the Finns exercising considerable diplomatic deftness. No matter how much the Soviet Union pressed them with its clumsy and immobile KGB machine, it could not compete with the nimble Finns, who were able to make faster decisions since there were only two or three gifted, intelligent and well-prepared statesmen involved. As a result Finland always outmanoeuvred the USSR with its giant collective brain. In my experience there is no such thing as 'collective intelligence', only 'collective stupidity'.

Another example of the benefits that springs from being a smaller unit is the ease with which quite important business can be conducted with informal efficiency. There were political customs in Finland that nobody talked about. Once a month, all political and trade union leaders gathered in a remote sauna near the capital – the so-called 'club'. They even invited communists and some of the most renowned businessmen. There they solved small problems of state to the interest of everybody. They realised that first of all they were Finns, then democrats, communists, fascists, or whatever. They had their differences, of course, but when it came to Finland, no one doubted even the loyalty of the communists! These meetings were organised so as not to waste society's energy on issues concerning national interest and they were possible because of the existing consensus in the name of their country, Finland. After leaving the sauna, they remained bitter rivals, they led political fights on all fronts, but it never crossed their minds to be more loyal to a foreign country than to their own, the way it was for a long time in Bulgaria in respect to the Soviet Union. Even less would they have sold or betrayed national interests for a ministerial chair.

There was a tradition in Finland, which probably still exists today, of 'House Russians'. The House Russian was a

Entering a Different World

counsellor or someone from the upper personnel of the Soviet embassy who was openly known to be a member of the KGB. His job was to develop a close and friendly relationship with a Finnish politician, minister or industrialist. The purpose of this arrangement was to avoid all the clumsy bureaucratic machinery and the long lines of official communication within the Soviet system that often didn't function effectively. Their existence allowed the wily Finns to outwit the Soviet system time and again.

The House Russians were appointed for their intelligence and supplied their masters with fast, accurate and fair information. They were usually people high up in the hierarchy with unlimited jurisdiction and, if they needed to, they could report directly to the Central Committee or the Politburo. There were jokes about them, saying that until you had your own House Russian you had not succeeded.

Dr Karjalainen and Kekkonen shared a House Russian who was the most important of them all, the legendary General Vladimirov. He had served four or five periods in the embassy as a chief counsellor, had spent most of his life in Finland and spoke the language perfectly. It was generally believed that he was the boss of all the Russian residents in Finland and Scandinavia since the KGB worked closely with the foreign ministry and most of the diplomats were spies, as was the case all over the world.

The first ambassador I worked for was Boris Nikolov, who made a stark contrast to the intelligence of General Vladimirov. He had been in Finland for a year by the time I arrived and had absolutely no idea why he was there or what an ambassador was meant to do. He had previously been a party secretary and was a simple-minded guy who treated his peers from other embassies the way he would have treated gypsies or Turks in his hometown. He patted them on the shoulder, pinched them good-naturedly and happily ate with

Fighting it Out

his fingers at official receptions. I had to interpret for him and although I was able to draw on my previous experience in leading conversations in order to cover the gaps in my ambassador's knowledge, it was impossible to fool experienced diplomats all the time. Our man made gaffe after gaffe, frequently leaving me scarlet with shame.

On one occasion we wanted to invite the world-famous Finnish architect and designer Alvar Aalto to a symposium in Varna. We went to the office of this charming old man and Nikolov immediately started patting him like a dog.

'Look here,' he bellowed, 'don't you know any Romanian or anything?'

The old man answered politely. 'I'm afraid I don't know Romanian, but I do speak Russian, Italian, French, Spanish, German, Portuguese, English and Swedish.'

'My God, what a stupid man,' our ambassador bellowed. 'Look at him! He can't speak even Romanian!'

I was too junior to do anything about the situation but others in the embassy wrote endless letters of complaint about him. Despite being a personal friend of Todor Zhivkov, he was eventually dismissed and replaced by Boris Hristov, an exceptional erudite, calm and well bred man with a long career in diplomacy, including the post of ambassador to Rome. My future father-in-law rated him highly, claiming that Bulgaria was 'too small a country for such a man'.

For eighteen months I lived from hand to mouth and nobody ever thought to give me any presents or 'see me right' as we say in Bulgaria. In the West, seeing myself right was my own problem. If I couldn't manage on my own, I had only myself to blame.

At that stage I imagined I would have a career in diplomacy. I envisaged finishing my time in Helsinki and then returning to Bulgaria with my young Finnish wife. From there we would be sent off to some new and exciting posting in another part of the

Entering a Different World

world. I was very happy with my lot in life. I was in love and I was out of Bulgaria, mixing with charming intelligent people.

Kukka-Maaria and I were married in December 1971 and I had to start thinking more seriously about my future. Was I really cut out for the diplomatic life? The other diplomats in the embassy had all been educated in Moscow, which gave them considerably greater opportunities. Officially or unofficially, the Soviet diplomatic school was the only recognised one. It was becoming obvious that I, with my provincial Bulgarian credentials, had little future in this field. The other consideration was Kukka-Maaria. Was it fair to ask her to go back to Bulgaria, away from her family to a country where she didn't speak the language and would find it very hard to make a career? Together we agreed that I had to leave the embassy and risk finding something for myself in the outside world. It was time to attempt to stand completely on my own two feet.

I shared my views with the ambassador.

'I think that is the most appropriate decision for a young man with prospects to make,' he said, without a hint of reproach in his voice. We wished each other good luck and parted company. I was now officially out of the Bulgarian system and starting a new life in the West, another leap into the unknown. To many in my home country I was now a traitor and for that I would never be forgiven.

Once out of the Embassy I had to adjust my ideas once more. All my life I had assumed I would be employed by the state. But I had now turned my back on the Bulgarian system and I could see the Finnish state was not about to give me a job. I had to look in the private sector, a sector I knew nothing about, a sector that didn't even exist in my own country. I'd been educated and groomed to be a communist leader, and now I had to think like a capitalist. Although the seeds of capitalist thinking had been sown in my mind by my

Fighting it Out

grandfather ever since I was old enough to listen, they had still never been nurtured or developed. I was now like a seedling that had been ripped up from its pot in the greenhouse and replanted in the unfamiliar soil of the garden, exposed to the elements for the first time, forced to put down strong roots if it was to survive.

Urgently needing a job, I approached the bosses of all the big companies in Finland, but none of them were interested. Why would they be interested in a young man, a junior diplomat from a foreign country with no business experience who didn't even speak Finnish? They were deeply suspicious, not surprisingly, of a man who did not speak their language fluently and carried a communist passport. I was going to have to try pulling strings again, but I was determined not to ask my father-in-law for help; I knew it was not the done thing.

One of the contacts I had made in the course of my work was the state secretary at the Finnish ministry of trade and industry. He was a man of Swedish descent called Bror Wahlroos. His was a non-political job, which he held regardless of which party was in power. He was a good man and he listened sympathetically to my story before promising to do what he could. But so unpromising did I seem as a potential employee that he couldn't persuade any of his contacts to even see me. The months slipped by and I began to wonder if I had made a mistake, and then he called me out of the blue.

'Go and see a man called Grotenfelt, he's the director of Finpap.'

I knew Finpap was the national union of Finnish paper producers, a commercial organisation for the trade and one of the biggest exporters in the world.

'He's from Swedish ancestry like me,' Bror explained, 'and he's about to leave the organisation and become the boss of Tampella.' Tampella was one of the biggest companies in the

Entering a Different World

country. 'He intends to reorganise the whole company and introduce some new blood.'

I did exactly as I was told, making my way to Mr Grotenfelt's office in the centre of Helsinki. There I found an exceptionally decent man and a towering figure. He ushered me into his office and took the time to listen to my story. I could sense there was a chemistry between us, although I hardly dared to believe it would lead to anything. When I had finished talking he took a deep breath and stared at me hard before replying.

'Listen to me, young man,' he said. 'Listen to me and you won't go wrong. I know what I'm talking about. I've travelled all over the world. My wife is Dutch and she's in Finland as a foreigner, just like you. It's very difficult here because this country is so isolated. There are hardly any foreigners and those that there are, are treated badly. I've been through it myself. So, the first thing you must do is become fluent in Finnish as quickly as possible. Secondly you must become a Finnish citizen immediately; otherwise you're lost!'

'I've only been here two years,' I replied. 'Doesn't the law require me to have been here at least three?'

'Work it out,' he said. 'Those are my conditions. There is no alternative.'

I went home deflated, and explained my predicament to Kukka-Maaria, knowing there was nothing to be done about gaining Finnish citizenship before the regulatory time. Having a prime minister for a father-in-law would mean nothing in Finnish law, I knew that. And the Finnish language! I already spoke five languages, but none of them had anything to do with Finnish. Even after two years I found it impossible to understand anything that was said to me, seeing no connections whatsoever to anything I already knew. On top of everything else the language has sixteen cases and exceptionally complicated grammar. Nobody outside the

Fighting it Out

country ever studied this language.

Kukka-Maaria listened to my defeatist talk and didn't even blink. 'Say "yes",' she said.

Her iron nerve gave me the necessary courage. After all, what did I have to lose? I rang Mr Grotenfelt the next day and told him I accepted his offer, or rather, his challenge.

'Come and see me in a month,' he replied. 'When I take charge of Tampella.'

A month later Kukka-Maaria and I were standing in front of the new president of one of the biggest concerns in the country. He was giving us his full attention, explaining the situation as he saw it to my wife.

'It will be extremely difficult for Atanas,' he said. 'He won't manage without your help. When I brought my wife here I protected her and introduced her into society, making it easier for her to adapt, but your situation is different. Atanas must provide for the family. This is why you must stay in Helsinki and continue with your studies. (She was doing her first major in economics.) I'm going to send your husband to a village two hundred kilometres away, to a factory that produces cardboard and paper. I'm going to ban everyone from talking to him in German or English. They'll only speak to him in Finnish. He'll have no choice.'

That was the deal. He would give me a job, but I had to do exactly what he told me. I had no choice but to accept and left immediately for the village, where I was more or less locked into two rooms with a pile of textbooks and dictionaries. I had no teachers or supervisors, only books and Finnish-speaking colleagues. I studied all day and in the evening I would ask any questions that were troubling me. The next day I would bury myself in the books again.

In order to speak a language fluently you need also to think in it. That means that when you are learning a language and have a limited vocabulary, you can only think with a limited

Entering a Different World

number of words, which changes the way you think and makes you feel stupid. It's a very disorientating experience, and one that I have had to go through several times in my life.

In three months I could still only speak pidgin Finnish, but it was something, and slowly, month upon month, I improved. While I was distracted by this mammoth task my third year of residence went by and I sent off my applications for Finnish citizenship to the Ministry of Internal Affairs.

There were endless formalities, including interviews and questions about being a communist spy or agent, culminating in one happy day in August when President Kekkonen made me a Finnish citizen by decree. I received a big seal covered with blue ribbons. It was the greatest joy in the world. The joy lasted until the middle of the following month, when I was called up to join the Finnish army.

I was stunned; just when I thought I had managed to escape from a regimented life, where I had to follow orders and do ridiculous time-wasting things just because I was told to, I was now going to have to start all over again with basic training. I was desperate to get going with my new life in the West, and I didn't want to start it off by waiting yet another year.

I went to see everyone I could possibly think of. I banged on the door of every institution that might see how ridiculous the situation was.

'I've been in the Bulgarian army for two years,' I explained, over and over again. 'I've sworn allegiance to the Warsaw Pact. I'm still answerable to them. If, God forbid, something should happen, whom should I fight for?'

They all nodded wisely, quite able to see my point, and then shrugged their shoulders; there was nothing they could do.

For the first time ever my father-in-law agreed to interfere. He could see this was an injustice and was willing to try to use his influence. He talked to the minister for defence and the chief of staff. They all agreed that this was the craziest way

Fighting it Out

imaginable of welcoming someone to Finland, but the law was the law. 'If you receive citizenship before the age of twenty-nine, you are obliged to serve!' I was one month away from my twenty-ninth birthday.

I was so incensed that for a moment I considered refusing citizenship, but eventually I saw sense. I had waited this long, overcome so many obstacles already, it would be foolish to give up at the last fence. There was no alternative; I had to get back out on that parade ground.

Apart from having to go all the way through basic training again, it wasn't too arduous a year. My job was to coordinate economic enterprises on military bases and it meant that by the end of the year, in 1974, my Finnish was fluent. Once more I was ready to start the glittering career that I had been dreaming about for so long.

During my national service I was moved to Tampere, the second largest town in Finland and the headquarters of the company I was going to be working for. Kukka-Maaria and I rented a small flat in town and the company agreed to pay half the rent. At least that showed they were willing to wait for me.

I believe that every so often in the course of your life the bird of luck will land on your shoulder. Without luck you can have the best ideas in the world, but the time you have on earth to make them a reality is finite. If you don't meet the right constellation of people to help you at the right time, if just one link in the chain is missing, nothing will happen. The important thing is to prepare yourself for that moment so that you recognise the bird when it arrives and do nothing to frighten it away. I knew that Mr Grotenfelt's offer was that bird and I was determined not to do anything to alarm it. Luck is also like love, if you stop working at it and take it for granted, you will soon lose it. Luck is a beautiful young bride and needs to be cherished.

CHAPTER SIX

CONQUERING RUSSIA

'I'm giving you the Soviet Union,' Mr Grotenfelt announced when I finally turned up for work, having carried out all his conditions, becoming a Finnish citizen and learning to speak the language like a native.

'I don't want to go there!' I said, horrified. I was deeply insulted. After all I had been through the last thing I wanted to do was go into the despised Soviet Union and work with the people who had destroyed my country and my family. I had nothing against any Russians individually, but the Soviet Bloc as a whole filled me with horror. Apart from that, I had also been looking forward to living and working in the West, with the efficiencies and comforts and opportunities that promised. The thought of having to go back to dealing with idiot communist bureaucrats was almost more than I could bear. Ever since I had become aware of life outside Bulgaria I had been looking towards the West. I had studied the languages, the cultures and the civilisations. I even liked the clothes. And now he was asking me to go back to the grey frustrating world I thought I'd escaped from.

Mr Grotenfelt had practically met me at the gates on the

Fighting it Out

day I was demobbed. He had great plans and wasn't going to be swayed. It didn't matter how much I protested at being sent to Russia, he had made up his mind. He wanted me to join a branch of the company called Tamrock, which produced some of the best mining machines in the world. Russia would be a new territory for the company, which was completely unknown in that market. It was a white spot on the map. He felt Russia had enormous prospects. I knew nothing about mining. I had never even been below ground. It sounded like a dark and dangerous industry to become involved in. He must have seen the horror written across my face.

'I'm giving you the Soviet Union because there's a saying in Finland,' he explained, 'that if you can succeed there, you can succeed anywhere. No company in Scandinavia strikes it rich without breaking into the Russian market. If you succeed the sky is the limit.'

I was not to be mollified, but I could see I had no choice and, once I had calmed down and thought about it logically, I could see it provided me with a tremendous opportunity to prove myself to the company. The little bird of luck was still there on my shoulder. 'The sky is the limit.' I would hold him to that promise one day.

Once I'd overcome my shock and disappointment, I brushed up my Russian, which I'd never had cause to actually use outside the classroom, and set off for Moscow. I told myself I would conquer this market quickly and then move on to more agreeable pastures. In my youthful ignorance I was feeling invulnerable once more.

The only time I'd been to Russia before was travelling on the train the first time I left Bulgaria for Finland. Life there was just as bleak and gloomy as I remembered from that journey. The more I got to know about Moscow the worse I realised the situation was. There were KGB agents round every corner, watching every move that anyone made, particularly foreigners

Conquering Russia

like me. The people were depressed and depersonalised. They would avoid making eye contact and do everything not to talk to any foreigner for fear of being pulled in for questioning. It was a totally closed society and I was definitely on the outside.

I knew it was a hard place to make a mark, but I was determined not to fail. I was always deeply committed to doing my best to realise whatever potential I had been born with. There is a joke that I particularly like, about a man appearing at the gates of heaven.

'You were a pious man,' St Peter says. 'What kind of reward do you want?'

'Well, I'm interested in history,' the man answers. 'Show me the greatest commander of all times and nations.'

St Peter delves into a chest and produces a bent old shoemaker.

'Wait a second,' the man says. 'I was expecting Alexander the Great or Napoleon! Who's this shabby old man?'

'We know those two you mentioned,' St Peter says, 'and many more. But this one was the greatest commander, only he did not understand his talent and failed to realise it.'

I was set on finding my talent, if I had one, and realising it. The optimism I felt can only be ascribed to my extreme youth and inexperience. It was only later, when I attended an advanced management course at Harvard, that I realised I had broken every business rule in the book during that period. At the time I didn't even know there was a book. If I had known, I dare say I would have given up and gone home. But I couldn't afford to go home; I had to justify Mr Grotenfelt's confidence in my abilities. If I gave up this challenge, the bird of luck might never come to roost on my shoulder again.

The machines I was attempting to sell were massive pieces of capital equipment, many of them as large as houses. The cheapest cost a million dollars and they went up to several times that. They provided the latest technology for drilling and

Fighting it Out

blasting, beating into rock faces at an incredible ten thousand blows a minute, creating holes four or five metres deep for the placing of explosives. They were awesome pieces of technology by anyone's standards.

Mining in the Soviet Union was a colossal industry, with between three and four million people going to work underground every day producing nickel, copper, diamonds and every other kind of metal and mineral. It provided a vast proportion of the wealth necessary to keep the Soviet empire going and make the lives of the party élite comfortable. There were also highways being built and tunnels being drilled through mountains.

The potential market for Tamrock's machines was unlimited, although there were three other foreign companies in the market. Atlas Copco, from Sweden, had been established in the market since the First World War, and two American companies had been there since the Second World War, when America was helping the Russians with their military effort. In my innocence I felt sure I would only have to make a few sales calls and I would start winning the business away from them.

One of the golden rules of business which I was to find out later on at Harvard is that if you are thinking of trying to break into a market, and 70 per cent of that market is divided up between two or three competitors, you should not attempt it because it is a hopeless case. A hundred per cent of the Soviet market was sewn up by three companies. I had absolutely no ideas and no plans, just enthusiasm and determination. There was no way that any experienced business person would have advised me to continue.

The equipment I was selling was good, but no better than the competition's. The service we could provide was also identical. There was no way we could undercut them on price because if we did come in below everyone else, in a market with very few customers, it would be almost impossible to get

Conquering Russia

the prices back up again and the business would be uneconomic even before we started. So the only way to differentiate the product was through the skills of the salesman, and there I was up against companies that had been in the market for over half a century. What sort of folly was this? To me, in my youthful ignorance, it seemed fine. All my life I have swum against the stream and whatever the rules may say, in order to succeed dramatically in life, you must be different. This is a skill no one can teach you, something that must come from within. If you're always swimming with the current you're exactly like everyone else, which gives you a very small chance of standing out.

Fired with this enthusiasm, and a certainty that if I could just prove myself here Mr Grotenfelt would soon be moving me on to greener pastures, I was able to turn a blind eye to the horrors of the unwelcoming hotels of Moscow, the endless waiting for food and transport and the ill-tempered officials who met you at every turn. All I had to do was locate the people who made the buying decisions, get in to see them and do the deals.

Always attracted by the unknown, I had discovered the power of yoga as a boy. I think I read about it first in a newspaper and set about digging out information wherever I could. Even at that early stage I found it had the most profound effect on me. In Moscow I found it invaluable. Exercising and relaxing are always hard for travelling business people. Yoga can be done in the privacy of a hotel room at any time of the night or day. I discovered that however tired and frustrated I became, half an hour of yoga would make a new man of me, both mentally and physically. Without it I think I might have ended up with a drink problem like so many of my colleagues. In the fifteen years I worked in Russia I had three engineers who had to leave because of drink problems.

'You don't have to drink every drop today;' I would caution

Fighting it Out

them, time after time, 'there will still be vodka left in Russia tomorrow.'

I started my one-man assault on the Russian mining industry by visiting the Finnish embassy and asking who they thought I should talk to. They told me there was an organisation that made all the buying decisions for machinery such as ours. This, I thought, was going to be easy. I only had to make one successful sale and I would be set up for life. The organisation in question was called Metalurgimport. This, I was told, was the only organisation with the right to trade in machines for the mining and building industries. They controlled the purchase of everything from the smallest drill bit to the largest metallurgical plant. They turned over tens of billions of dollars every year. The embassy gave me the telephone number and I returned to my dingy hotel room and the inefficient Moscow telephone system. Eventually, after battling for some hours with broken connections, bored operators and unhelpful juniors, I was given the name Dronnov. This man, apparently, was responsible for commercial supplies. He was the man I had to target. There was no other.

Relieved that I was finally on the road forward I made the call. Dronnov answered with a grunt.

'My name is Tilev,' I announced proudly. 'I'm calling from a company called Tampella-Tamrock. I would like to come and negotiate with you.'

'I've never heard of Tampella-Tamrock,' he snapped back. 'I do not want to know you and I have nothing to talk to you about.' He hung up the phone.

I tried again, several times, but got nowhere. This man had all his suppliers set up and running. Why would he be interested in making work for himself by changing to someone new? What interest did he have in forging a new relationship with some unknown young man who thought he was God's gift to selling? Even if Tamrock's machines were better than their rivals and would save the authorities money by improving productivity, why would he care? His salary would still be the same whatever deal he did. Nothing I had to say could have been of interest to a man sitting at a desk in an anonymous office. All he was interested in was making as little effort as possible.

I reported back to Grotenfelt, saying that it looked as if the market was already sewn up. He did not think that was reasonable grounds for giving up.

'Keep trying,' he instructed. 'We have to break into this market.'

I thought a little more deeply about the problem. I knew that if I was not going to be able to impress Mr Dronnov, I was going to have to get round him to the people who really made the decisions, the people who actually knew about mining and were interested in their subject. I understood enough about the communist system to know that the bureaucrats sat at the front of everything, slowing things down with their idleness, ignorance and stupidity, but that behind them there were still people of quality working in every industry. These people would be as frustrated by the weight of the state and the slowness of the bureaucracy as I was, and if they could be enthused by the Tamrock machines, they would insist that they be ordered. Since Mr Grotenfelt obviously wasn't going to let me come home until I had succeeded, I set about finding these people.

I knew that Mr Dronnov was no more than an instrument for buying. The decisions on what was actually needed by the industry were taken by the Ministry of Foreign Trade. They had set up Mr Dronnov's company simply to buy equipment connected to the metallurgy industry. It was not his own money he was spending. I needed to get to the people who actually had the money. I was pretty sure that my competitors,

Fighting it Out

having managed to win the attention of Mr Dronnov, had not felt the need to delve any further into the hierarchy.

When I investigated further I found that it was like a false mirror. Mr Dronnov was the visible reflection, but behind the mirror sat the people who actually told him what to do. They were people at places like the Ministry of Non-Ferrous Metals, the Ministry of Transport Construction, the Ministry for Energy Construction and the Ministry for Coal. All these people needed to buy mining equipment for different reasons, and they hired Mr Dronnov to do it for them.

I started visiting the ministries and found intelligent pragmatic people who were always willing to listen to anyone who had ideas for how they could do their work better and more efficiently. They had plans they wanted to fulfil and I knew how to talk to them. Whereas my competitors were just selling and going home, I got to know people and tried to think of a way of doing business which would work better for them as well as for us. There had to be a different way of approaching the whole business.

I was not the only person arriving in Moscow and trying to win business from the Russians in those days, and the drudgery of the work drove many of my fellow businessmen to drink and worse. In the end, however hard you worked and however intelligent and well educated you were it always came back to the little bird of luck as to whether or not you would succeed. It was pure luck that I had met Mr Grotenfelt and that he had seen something in me which he thought he could use. It also was pure luck that I had met Kukka-Maaria and moved to Finland. In Moscow I struck lucky once more. I made contact with people in the Ministry of Transport Construction (Mintransstroi) and the Ministry of Non-Ferrous Metallurgy (Mintsvetmet), and for some reason I could not work out, they decided they liked me. There was certainly a great deal of sweat and determination needed to get to meet them, but it was simply good fortune that they decided I was a person they wanted to deal with.

The second golden rule of doing business in a new market is to go armed with references. I had none. The company was new; I was new. We had only just arrived in the market. Where would I get references? Once again a wiser business head would have realised the futility of the venture and gone home. The communists are a very suspicious breed. They are not risk takers. They want to be sure before they commit themselves to any sort of contract. Doing business with an unknown such as myself was a big risk for them to take.

My contacts advised me to travel to the mines and actually meet the workers and engineers who would operate the machines I was selling. I took their advice and flew with them to Tashkent. It was October and the weather was sunny. Several cars were waiting for us at the airport and we were driven six hundred kilometres out into the desert. The local people had never seen a foreigner before since a veil of military secrecy covered the whole area and meant that outsiders never normally got to go there. It seemed I was being honoured in some way by this invitation.

We stopped in Chimkent to view the giant red brick mosque (the size of St Paul's Cathedral) that Timur Lenk, the grandson of Genghis Khan, had built for his mistress, before driving on another two hundred kilometres to Kentau, a town in the middle of the desert, sitting upon colossal deposits of copper and nickel. Every day more than 150,000 people from the town would go underground to work. Where not long ago there had been nothing but a few tents in the sand, there were now mighty blocks of Soviet-style apartments to house these people and their families, and the water pumped up from the mines meant there were also trees in this gigantic oasis.

The party secretary and the rest of the managers were lined up to meet the guests from Moscow. After being shown round the mines to see how they were using the existing machines, we were invited for a walk and a rest on the side of an artificial lake that the authorities had built. I noticed there were a great many cotton fields along the edges of the town and was impressed that they had been able to create such elaborate irrigation in the desert. When we reached the lake, however, I realised how they had done it. There was not a single drop of water left, nothing but dead fish on baked mud. A plan that must have looked so promising on the drawing board had turned into a disaster in reality.

At two o'clock that afternoon we started to eat and drink at a feast that lasted until six o'clock the following morning. Every two hours we were given a break of fifteen or twenty minutes to get some fresh air. During that time the table was cleared and reset with fresh food so that we could start all over again. As the chief guest I had to reply to every toast, raise my glass and drink to everyone, one by one, downing the vodkas in one swallow.

At one stage my hosts placed a roast lamb in the middle of the table and I had to poke its eye out and eat it, together with the attached nerves. When they explained to me what was expected I felt a wave of nausea rising up inside me. I fought it back; there was no way out of this without insulting my hosts, the people upon whom my entire future rested. Playing for time, I stood up and made a long speech, explaining how happy I was to be there, how privileged to be the guest of such fine people, and sincerely thanking them for the honour of being able to poke out the eye. Then I had a brainwave: I pointed out that it was too great an honour for one man and suggested we should share it. Working quickly so I didn't have to think about what I was doing, I stabbed the eye out, cut it into small pieces and passed them round. I placed my piece in my mouth and swallowed it, like a pill, with another glass of vodka. Face had been saved and the party continued.

By then I was aware of just how fast the vodka flowed at these gatherings and I had come armed with two bottles of Alka-Seltzer. In each of the breaks I took three or four tablets and somehow that kept me going. I got drunk, there was no question about that, but more slowly than everyone around me. By five o'clock in the morning I was the only man standing; the rest lay sprawled on the floor around me. The party secretary was underneath the table but still conscious.

'Come here,' he shouted to the cook, 'and drink with the devil!'

The devil apparently was me, and I then had to drink with the cook as well.

As dawn broke the sprawled mass of bodies stirred into life and we were loaded back into the cars and taken away. That afternoon they wanted to start the party all over again with a drinking competition to see if my luck had been a fluke.

'You respect us, don't you?' they asked when I protested at the idea of punishing my stomach any further.

'Of course I do,' I replied indignantly. 'Didn't I show that already?'

I somehow convinced them to leave me alone and to hold their drinking competition the following day, after I had left for the six-hundred-kilometre journey back to the airport. As a farewell gesture we drank three vodkas each on empty stomachs. The Russians who were to accompany me and who were still thirsty, loaded ten bottles into the car for the journey. They tried to press more on me in the car but I was resolute. I knew I had reached my limit. Eventually they realised I was serious and kept the drink to themselves, passing it back and forth to the driver as we sped across the desert. Soon the driver was so drunk he lost all sense of direction.

'Here Tashkent. There Tashkent. No Tashkent!'

By the time we finally arrived at the airport, the plane had long gone.

Fighting it Out

'Big deal,' they said, patting me happily on the back. 'We will sit here in the VIP lounge and live like kings until the next flight.'

'That's all very well,' I said, 'but my visa expires tonight.'

I could see them struggling through the haze of vodka to cope with this new piece of information. To have a Westerner with them in Tashkent without a visa was serious indeed. It would be bad for me to be caught but even worse for them; they could all lose their jobs. As the fog cleared from their brains panic replaced it. They found the airport commandant and told him I was the personal delegate of President Kekkonen of Finland, a fully-fledged ambassador. The commandant realised the urgency of the situation and started making calls, searching for the plane. He eventually discovered it a thousand kilometres away on its way to Moscow. Making contact with the captain on the radio, he ordered him back to Tashkent.

I waited on the tarmac, my two suitcases beside me, as, a few hours later, the plane landed. I watched as a ladder was brought and four people marched aboard, two in uniform and two civilians. They grabbed the first person they came to, sitting by the door, and threw him off without so much as a please or a thank you, ushering me into his seat. As the plane took off once more I looked out the window and saw the poor man standing on the runway, blinking in bemusement. The little bird of luck had certainly deserted him that day.

I visited other mines in those months, including one that lay right on the edge of the Arctic Circle. It was a huge concern in an area where it was dark for six months of the year and frostbound all the time. Over a million people lived in and around that mine. It might not have been an economically viable business – at least it wouldn't have been if all those people had been being paid a living wage – but it was an immense achievement by anyone's standards.

Conquering Russia

As I got to know the people in charge of the industry better, it occurred to me that we needed to find a way to cement the relationship if I was ever going to be able to sell to them. I needed to give them a stake in the machines that would make it completely non-viable for them to buy from any of the competition. I had no way of taking business from their established suppliers in the normal way. I had to make a quantum leap in my thinking and come up with an idea that would put us in a league of our own, offering them something that none of the competitors had even thought about.

Then it came to me. I suggested that we set up a joint venture enterprise with them. We at Tamrock would provide the expertise and they, the Russians, would do the actual manufacturing. In any market where the competing products are similar and these days most competent companies can make most products if they want to the only way to win is in the selling, which means coming up with new ideas.

'I don't want to sell you anything,' I said with bravado. 'I want to help you produce the machines for yourselves here. It'll be much more cost-effective for you. You'll save money; we'll save money; everyone'll be happy.'

Unfortunately, I had not actually put the idea to my own company, knowing they would be reluctant to embrace it and wanting to get the Russians on board before presenting it at home. I was speaking totally without the authority needed to make my promises a reality. At that time no one in the West wanted to make these sorts of deals with the Soviet Union, fearful that if they started giving their secrets to the Russians, they would steal them and make the products themselves. The suspicion between East and West was so great that any suggestion of releasing technical information was met with horror. In Finland the reaction was even worse than it might have been in America or Sweden. The Finns and the Russians had been at war twice within living memory. Understandably,

Fighting it Out

there was a great deal of mutual suspicion. But I knew how the Soviet Union worked. I knew that even if they did steal the plans they were not equipped to do anything with them. They simply weren't technologically competent enough to pose a threat.

My colleagues in Helsinki were all set to lynch me when I told them the deal I had come up with. It has been my experience that it is often harder to sell good ideas on how to do things differently to your own people than it is to sell any to your customers. There are reasons for this, including bureaucracy, infighting, inertia and competing strategies. I explained to them that the Russians were incapable of stealing their ideas; that this way Tamrock would be saved the work of making the machines and would be able to concentrate on the most profitable part of the operation, the technology. It would provide a positive interdependence between our customer and us.

'But they're sending people into space,' my detractors argued. 'How can you say they're technologically incompetent?'

'That's the military,' I replied. 'This is industry. There's an iron wall between the two sectors. Nothing the military does ever filters through to the industrial sector; they're too secretive. I may not know much about mining, but I know a lot about Soviet culture.'

My close colleagues at Tamrock were as reluctant as everyone else to make this deal, telling me I would never be able to cope with the complications of a joint venture. I could see I wasn't going to win them over so I concentrated my efforts on persuading Mr Grotenfelt that it would give us the whole market on a plate.

'OK,' he said, overruling all the people who were carping about minor details. 'I'll send the lawyers in and we'll look at the possibilities.'

'No,' I said, horrified. 'If you send the lawyers in they'll never agree to anything. We just have to do it. The Russians have to see that we trust them. Once you've won the trust of a good Russian he'll be your friend for life. They won't betray us if we act fairly with them.'

Luckily for me Mr Grotenfelt was a man after my own heart, someone willing to take a few risks if the potential rewards were good enough. He nodded. 'All right,' he said. 'Do it.'

If I had not had his support at that moment the deal would never have been done and Tamrock would never have become anything. Because of his foresight and courage it would become the leading concern in its field in the world. By letting me give away the company's secrets he put his head on the block alongside my own.

The boss at the purchasing department of Mintsvetmet, with whom I wanted to build this joint enterprise, listened to my suggestion once I was empowered to make it official. 'You're an interesting case,' he said. 'A foreigner all alone in the Valley of Death, and from Slavic origins at that! We'll help you for nothing, just to see what happens.'

Once I had them on my side, Mr Dronnov was little more than an inconvenience. He might ring around the competition and try to get the prices down a bit, but there wasn't much else he could do. Once I had the ministry people on board, little could stop me. Nothing however happens overnight, particularly in Russia. Before they were willing to start a joint venture, they wanted to try the machines out. An order was placed with Tamrock for one machine, and then another and another. It seemed I was in with a chance, although I knew I could be squeezed out just as quickly if things went against me.

Inevitably, my contacts did not have the final say in whether the plan went ahead. Above the ministries in the hierarchy, above even the Ministry of Finance, was an organisation called Gosplan, which laid plans for the entire Soviet economy and allocated money to different projects. They tended to fund things

Fighting it Out

for five years at a time and every ministry always asked for more than it needed to give itself room for negotiation. Any submission to Gosplan had to be well founded and well explained by specialist lobbyists. It was a long and complicated procedure, but it meant that all the time we were waiting they were testing our machines and getting to know us better. Over the next four years, from 1974 to 1978, they bought four hundred million dollars' worth of machines from Tamrock. Once they were happy with us and with the equipment, they agreed to set up the joint venture.

In a town called Kamengorsk, in the middle of Kazakhstan, we started to assemble machines in 1975. Seventy per cent of each machine was our property, but the Russians saved up to thirty per cent of the import value – a sizeable amount of money – and felt they had more control over their own destiny. Our engineers went out there for months at a time to help them set up. When Tamrock's chief engineer arrived at the factory for the first time with a team of Finns to help them with the product cycle, he found himself met by several thousand workers. They ate and drank to future success for three days and nights. On the fourth day they escorted him to the huge manufacturing premises where an enormous red carpet had been laid out, leading to a large red armchair in the midst of all the machines, lathes and factory dirt.

'Sit here,' they told him, 'and if we need anything we'll ask you.'

We produced only three different types of machines on the premises, the rest continued to be sold directly from Finland. By providing them with all the technical information they needed, enough for all their universities and training establishments, we made Tamrock machines the industry standard. Within a very short time we had a hundred per cent of the Russian market and had driven our deeply established competitors out. Hundreds of millions of dollars of profits started pouring in from a business that just a couple of years before had not existed. By the time the competition had woken up to what we were doing and tried to copy us, it was too late. By 1980 we had a complete monopoly.

The commercial relationship between Finland and the Soviet Union had been developed with great intelligence in the years since the war, using a system of clearing payments that benefited the Finns enormously. This meant that the free currency was hardly used and there were two accounts at the central banks of both parties with each state paying their exporters in local currency. Finland bought mainly crude oil and resources from the USSR, paying in roubles for commodities that they would have to pay for in dollars anywhere else in the world, and they sold back those same resources, processed and at much higher prices, in their own currency. The profits were huge. I participated in some of these deals and I know that the figures stretched beyond imagination.

As the years passed Russia did not become any easier to work in, and after every trip I swore I would never go back. But once the money started to come in, life in Moscow became more comfortable. Once we had convinced the Ministry of Foreign Trade that their country needed us, we were allowed to open our own offices. The bleak hotel rooms were replaced with large conference rooms, dining rooms and private apartments. There were saunas and chauffeurs, cocktail parties and cooks to take some of the pain out of being in such an oppressed country. I still made sure I never stayed there for more than a couple of weeks at a time; I had seen too many foreigners becoming depressed and taking to drink or compromising themselves with prostitutes out of sheer boredom. I went home at regular intervals.

My brother came over to Moscow to work with me, bringing his wife and children, which meant I actually had

Fighting it Out

family I could visit in the long evenings. The people I met within the ministries began to become close friends. My circle of contacts included ministers, heads of department, engineers and experts of every type. I was enormously impressed by the abilities of many of them and by the way they managed to continue working under the most difficult of circumstances.

Although the business was growing beyond my wildest expectations and I had made many good friends, I still found Moscow a depressing place. Every time I got back to Helsinki I would complain to Mr Grotenfelt, asking to be moved to a new area.

'I haven't spent all these years studying just to do this,' I told him.

'All right, my man!' He said eventually in 1978. 'Let's find you some more virgin territory.' He made a show of looking at a map of the world. 'Ah, the Far East. There you go, everything from Japan, through South Korea and Taiwan to the Philippines. It's all yours. You've got six months to prepare yourself.'

Once again I was being given a white spot, virgin territory where nobody would have heard of Tamrock or Tampella, where they might even have difficulty locating Finland or Bulgaria on a map. I was being launched back into the unknown, a complete outsider, hunting again, and I loved it.

CHAPTER SEVEN

CONQUERING THE FAR EAST

Although Japan was the second largest economic power in the world, Tampella had not sold a single screw there. I was starting from scratch and needed to find out as much as possible about the country and its people, starting with its history and literature. I was going to need the six months Mr Grotenfelt had allocated in order to learn enough about the culture to be able to make an impact. No one was going to take any notice of me if I turned up behaving like an American tourist. The Japanese are a proud people. They are particularly impressed by foreigners who can talk about their writers, their art and their customs; they never want to talk solely about business.

I read everything I could lay my hands on about Japan, while at the same time continuing to oversee our Russian operation. I knew it would be impossible for me to master the Japanese language, which was totally different to any of the languages I already knew, but did do everything else I could to understand them and their way of thinking.

I discovered that the Japanese are masters of understatement. You can see the evidence in their literature,

Fighting it Out

their architecture and design. The Nobel Prize winner, Kawabata, for instance, has written several books; enormous pieces of work, all sketches and allusions. They leave great space for the imagination and imply truths that are barely touched upon in more voluminous novels. Their Haiku poetry is also extremely frugal: a word or two, an image, a metaphor. But your imagination is presented with a limitless field of vision, your mind set free of all kinds of dogmas and prejudices. In their architecture the apparent understatement reveals an aesthetic modesty, as sometimes seen in good modern Italian and Scandinavian furniture. It is stripped of superfluous detail and pomposity and is simple and light. I learnt from the Japanese that in all matters – speech, gesture design or building it is better to use skilful restraint so that there is order and empty space. There's great wisdom in understatement.

This was in marked contrast to everything Russian and was going to be a very different market to break into, requiring very different social skills. Here there was no state bureaucracy, everything was privately owned. The barriers here would be that as a nation the Japanese wanted only to sell to the outside world, not to buy from it. It was a deliberate policy. The Ministry of Industry and Trade had made long-term plans for the protection of the Japanese market. I was also coming to the market once more without references, since my success in Russia would mean nothing to them.

Although I wanted to set up a joint production facility just as we had in the Soviet Union, I also wanted to sell other products from the Tampella group into the Far East, including textiles for the interior refurbishment of hotels. I had a Japanese friend I had met in Finland called Satoshi. He had come to Finland to study architecture and had married a Finn. He later became wealthy by importing wooden blockhouses into Japan from Finland.

Fighting it Out

With my parents at Morska Gradina Park in Varna, aged 3.

Fighting it Out

The way I started.

With my brother Valentin, centre and my parents, in Sofia, during the winter of 1970.

A fright for the enemies of the Bulgarian army – with Private Spassov (*right*), on military service, 1964.

With Kukka-Maaria on a break near Varna in 1968 – our lives ahead of us.

Fighting it Out

▶ At the Soviet Ministry of Non-Ferrous Metallurgy in Moscow, 1981, with Deputy Minister Novikov (*centre*), Gribovsky (*on far left*), Bushuev and Grotenfelt (*right*).

▼ At the highest level: myself (*far right*) accompanying President Kekkonen of Finland (*right of centre*) and Prime Minister Alexei Kosygin of the Soviet Union (*facing, left*) on a visit to Tampella, 1975.

Fighting it Out

Fighting it Out

In my chequered suit, delivering an impromptu lecture to Egor Ligachev, President Gorbachev's deputy and second most important man in the Soviet Union, 1987.

With the President of Tampella, L. Vatinen, signing a major contract in Moscow, 1994.

At the inauguration of the Rover car assembly plant in Varna, with the President of Bulgaria, Dr. Ghelio Ghelev (*left*) and the Minister of State in Britain's Department of Trade and Industry, Lord Ferrers, in 1995.

At the inauguration of the yoghurt factory in Beijing, 1996. Some of the Chinese partners pictured went on to steal the money and ruin the factory.

Fighting it Out

Fighting it Out

◀ With my son Harri, and daughters Maria (*r*) and Kristina (*l*), in Bulgarian traditional dress, 1983.

▼ With Nils Grotenfelt at his country estate in Juva, 1982.

Fighting it Out

With King Simeon (*right*) Kukka-Maaria (*behind the King*), Doña Margarita; and my daughters Maria (*l*), and Kristina (*r*),

Fighting it Out

With HRH King Simeon (*right*), in 1982.

Fighting it Out

Three generations at the midsummer fire at a lake in Finland in 1986: (*left to right, back row*) Paivi, Ahti, Kukka-Maaria, (*front row*) Harri, Maria and Kristina.

Conquering the Far East

As I talked to Satoshi about his country I discovered he'd been sponsored to travel by a man called Yoshiaki Tsutsumi. Before long I had found out that this man was one of the richest in Japan. He owned more than a hundred top-grade hotels, but they were only a minor part of his business interests. He came from an eminent family and was close to the imperial court. When the Americans took away the emperor's income after the Second World War, Tsutsumi's father had financed the imperial family. After the Korean War, the Americans needed a powerful ally in the area and decided to put Japan back on its feet. They returned the emperor's huge wealth and Tsutsumi's loyalty was rewarded with royal patronage.

It seemed that the little bird of luck had landed on my shoulder once again. I could never have planned to meet someone who had access to such a powerful man, such a thing could only happen by serendipity. I knew I must move very slowly and quietly if I was not to startle this bird and frighten it away.

The mentality of the Japanese is closer to that of the Balkans than to Finns. Those who have money are expected to show it off. Living and working in Tokyo, however, was nothing like being in Moscow or Stara Zagora. This was one of the richest, most cultured and exciting cities on earth, where everyone was out to work as hard as they could and be as successful as possible.

The first morning I was in Tokyo I came down to breakfast at the Okura hotel, one of the finest in the world. All the tables were occupied and so I asked an elderly American if I might join him. As we got talking he asked me how long I had been in the country and I confessed I'd come in the previous night. He told me he'd been there since the war.

'Son,' he said, 'are you like all the idiots who come here knowing nothing and preaching Western ways?'

Fighting it Out

I assured him I wasn't and explained how much trouble I had taken to prepare myself.

'I can see you'll succeed,' he said after a while. 'But I'll give you a tip on how to deal with the Japanese. When you get into close contact with them, in your mind's eye you need to take off their blue suits and dress them instead in traditional kimonos, with a sword on each hip. Then you'll have a better idea of the sort of men you're dealing with.'

His words proved to be wise; he had encapsulated the differences between our cultures. He'd summed up the Japanese mentality of 'us against the world'. They believed they were God's chosen nation and would only buy something if it were to their advantage. They were bound by tight traditional codes of behaviour and honour that had to be respected by anyone who wanted to do business with them.

It proved much easier to open a few doors and start talking to people than it had been in Moscow, but it was just as hard to persuade them to actually sign up. The Japanese policy of exporting as much as possible and importing as little as possible might have infuriated the rest of the world, particularly America, who saw it as unfair trading, but it was making Japan very rich indeed and they did not intend to change their ways until they had to.

When Mr Grotenfelt decided to come out with me to see how things were going, I asked my friend Satoshi if he could arrange a meeting for us with his sponsor, the powerful Yoshiaki Tsutsumi. Such meetings could not be set up over night and we had to wait three days before we were finally ushered into a great hall about three hundred square metres in size. The only furniture was a few cushions on the floor. On the walls were six original Picassos; in the waiting room outside the hall we had seen a letter addressed to Tsutsumi's father, the characters written by the emperor. This, we knew, was almost like a blessing from above. The writing of characters in Japan is considered high art, and to have some executed by the emperor himself was worth any number of Picassos.

Mr Grotenfelt, president of one of the biggest companies in northern Europe, and I were invited to sit on the cushions and some extremely polite girls brought us green tea to sip while we waited – for four hours. At the end of the fourth hour Tsutsumi San entered the room, said 'Good day' and enquired who we were. Someone explained and he nodded his understanding. With no negotiation or discussion he told us he would like us to refurbish three of his hotels, regardless of price. He gave each of us a watch and then left the hall. The meeting, which we had travelled across the world for, had lasted no more than four minutes, but it had been worth the journey. Knowing Tsutsumi opened every door to us in the Far East and we were able to start our hunt for a partner in earnest.

To set up offices in all the Far East markets would have cost us millions of dollars, with no guarantee that we would succeed in selling a thing. If we could persuade one of the Japanese trading giants to act as our representative, we would not have to make any investment at all; the entire infrastructure would already be in place. It took us two years and six or seven visits before we persuaded Mitsui to represent us.

Mitsui is one of the world's most powerful trading companies, with an annual turnover of more than a hundred billion dollars. They were funding huge projects all over the world, not just in the Fast East but also in South America and the Third World, even in Bulgaria, where they were building underground power stations in the mountains. Mitsui would agree to loan governments the money for these capital-intensive projects, on the understanding that they provided the equipment. Since Mitsui didn't want to manufacture the equipment themselves, they would allow us to supply it. Mitsui would effectively lend the client the money to pay for our machines, doing all our marketing for us. It worked perfectly

Fighting it Out

and soon we were selling hundreds of millions of dollars' worth of equipment through them every year.

When added to the success of the Russian market, the Mitsui contract meant that Tamrock was now a worldwide giant. Although I had been supported at every step by Mr Grotenfelt, I had achieved this on my own, a fact that I was extremely proud of. I had created a mighty profit-making machine through a mixture of luck, foresight, meeting the right people at the right time and being able to distinguish what was important from what was unimportant. The rewards were commensurate with my success. I was now appointed commercial director and given all the offices, secretaries and company cars I would need. I was earning a salary which I would never have dared to dream of when I was living in my cupboard in the Helsinki embassy and I was travelling all the time.

Tampella employed more than fifteen thousand people and, as in any company, there was fierce internal competition for the few top jobs. There was no shortage of people watching my progress and asking themselves why an immigrant from Bulgaria was achieving so much success. Since envy is not a characteristic of my own countrymen, I was surprised to find myself up against a hissing biting wall of envious people within Tampella who seemed to want nothing better than to bring me down. They whispered about how I lacked education and how Bulgarians were only ever taught to buy and sell things, not how to run giant businesses. Although I knew I had the full support of my president, I also knew that I was on very thin ice indeed. If anything happened to Mr Grotenfelt I would be destroyed by the mob in a matter of weeks. I had to do something to strengthen my position and make myself independent so that, should the worst happen, I would be equipped to move to a similar job in another corporation.

I went to see Mr Grotenfelt and told him how my colleagues were insulting me and how they seemed to want to tear me apart.

'Pay no attention,' he said, patting me consolingly on the shoulder. 'You're our golden boy.'

'That may be true,' I said, 'but I don't want them to be able to call me nothing but a buyer and seller. I want you to send me to study.'

'Study where?'

'At Harvard. They run a course you can attend if you have a degree and a world-class company sponsoring you and guaranteeing your future career.'

'I don't think it's that simple,' he said. 'Competition for places on those courses is fierce.'

'I know,' I said. 'But if you'll give me your support I'll see if there are any other strings I can pull.'

For the second time in my life I went to my father-in-law for help. I didn't want money from him, just a recommendation to the US ambassador to Finland, a lady called Rosanne Ridgeway. Having set the wheels in motion I went back to work in Finland and, when I least expected it, which seems to be the way most good things happen, my secretary rang to tell me I had been accepted by Harvard. It was a moment of enormous joy for me.

Having started with a rather formal relationship, my father-in-law and I had become close. The Karjalainen family were incredibly tactful and they never showed the slightest doubt about their daughter marrying me, although they must have harboured all the usual parental worries. Once they had decided I was not a cheap opportunist, but a decent, hard-working and educated guy who had managed to find his own way in life, we trusted each other completely.

Dr Karjalainen was an extremely intelligent man. In 1939, during the war with Russia, he volunteered for the army; he was barely sixteen. At its conclusion he went home for a short while and then the Second World War broke out and he went back to the front for the rest of the conflict. After the war he studied economics and finance and began working as a journalist. He then joined the Bank of Finland and never officially left. There he wrote his doctorate on currency finance and, quite by accident, met with Kekkonen, who changed his life. He entered politics, a career path he had never imagined for himself.

He never had anything to do with the sort of cheap politics that dominate the newspapers of every Western country. He had an exceptionally solid education and was enormously cultured, with a rich variety of interests including literature, the history of art and music. He was considered a genius by many and in politics was a super heavyweight. He was always restrained in public, and even with his family he did not speak a lot, but each word was chosen carefully. He popularised a saying: 'Think what you say to avoid saying what you think.'

As our relationship developed we went on holiday together several times, just the two of us. We visited Greece, Italy, and Yugoslavia and once went to his old friend Patolitchev's villa in Sochi. Patolitchev was minster of foreign trade for the Soviet Union for thirty years. He was a member of the Central Committee of the Communist Party and co-chairman of the Soviet-Finnish Economic Council. He and my father-in-law were the architects of the business relationship which had done so much to ensure the prosperity of modern Finland.

The first time Dr Karjalainen introduced me to Patolitchev was in Moscow. The Russian seemed a shy, easy-going man. When he first saw me he said, 'So this is him?'

'Yes, this is him.' Dr Karjalainen nodded.

'Where do you work?' he asked me.

'Tampella,' I replied.

'Ah,' he laughed. 'Very good. You need to work for big companies and with big capitalists. There's nothing worse than a poor capitalist!'

He sent us straight to Sochi where we stayed for a week. Although he spoke German, English, French and Swedish, my father-in-law spoke little Russian and we had to have interpreters.

On one of my earliest business trips to Moscow, when I knew no one and used to wander from hotel to hotel in search of diversion and congenial company, I met two dark, bearded fellows. One of them turned out to be the first secretary of the Greek embassy and the other a Cypriot. They lived in the diplomatic housing estate opposite the Ukraine Hotel and had spent more than ten years in Moscow. Finding out that my father-in-law and I would be going on holiday to Greece, the Greek one, who we called Harry, arranged a meeting for us with Averov, the deputy prime minister at the time. We had not intended visiting anyone, but we could not say no. Averov arranged a helicopter to take us to Delphi, 'the centre of the world'. According to Greek mythology, Zeus released two eagles, each with a big stone in its beak, in opposite directions to find out where the centre of the world was. When they bumped into each other they dropped the stones, in Delphi.

'Well,' my father-in-law mused when he heard the story, 'the Finns think that the centre of the world is Finland.'

Averov was an engaging companion. He, Dr Karjalainen and I spent some very enjoyable times together and I have particularly warm memories of stormy nights in small tavernas, dancing the *sirtaki* and smashing plates according to the local custom.

Back in Helsinki he and I would spend endless hours in conversation, and sometimes I would persuade him to come jogging or swimming with me. I learnt a lot from him about life and people, and I also learnt from his humility. You cannot learn to be wise, humble and welcoming; it has to come from inside. He never had any guards and when he walked the streets alone he would stop and talk with the same kindness and consideration to drunkards at the dockside as to the kings and queens he met officially. There was nothing false, no theatre, no posing, not a drop of the populism that is so clearly to be seen in mediocre politicians. The closer I came to him, however, the more I felt his loneliness.

CHAPTER EIGHT

A COMPLETE IDIOT

'Is this true?' one of the doctors at Harvard, a psychiatrist, asked, riffling through my papers. 'You started working at Tamrock five years ago and now your profits are supporting nearly the whole business?'

We had just completed some psychological tests and analyses and the doctor had phoned me and asked to meet.

'Yes, it's true,' I replied, puzzled by his tone. The point of the tests, as I understood, was to assess our strengths and weaknesses so that the university could make recommendations to our sponsoring companies.

'In that case, Mr Tilev,' he said, 'I must put it bluntly to you, that you are a complete idiot!'

That was not what I had been expecting to hear. I had been feeling rather pleased with myself. Not only had I been accepted onto the course at Harvard, but when I got there I found that I was the youngest participant by ten years and that all the others were senior executives running global companies, many of which were household names. I was by far the newest kid on the block. So how could it be that I was a complete idiot?

Harvard University is the citadel of the political economic theory of capitalism. Along with Stanford and Yale it is one of

Fighting it Out

the most eminent universities of the United States. Its contribution has been to translate theory into practice and as a result it has had an enormous impact on the political and economic life of the United States, and consequently the whole modern world.

Harvard is the brains trust of the US government. There are a number of task forces in the university which, on a daily basis, provide the political and administrative management of the country with alternative solutions to economic, industrial and international relations issues. Harvard professors make up around 75 per cent of the personnel of a number of key ministries, defining their goals, suggesting their strategies and methods for attaining them. The bosses of many of the most powerful banks and companies, as well as the specialists who work for them, are graduates of Harvard.

The six-month course I was attending was in upper management and there were students from all over the world being trained in the fundamentals of economy, cash flows, economic processes and the environment of the big corporation. So how could I, who had been accepted for a course by these people, be a complete idiot?

'Anyone with any intelligence,' the doctor went on, 'finding themselves in your position, would leave the company, become an independent representative and work for a percentage. You should be a rich man, Mr Tilev, not just a well paid one.'

It seems obvious now, with the benefit of hindsight, but at the time I was deeply loyal to Mr Grotenfelt and Tampella. I had also come from a socialist country where private property was a theoretical notion and my understanding of wealth was to find a job, become a boss as quickly as possible and be paid a handsome salary. I had achieved all that. I had all the credit cards and unlimited expense accounts. I had thought I was doing pretty well, but now I could see that my whole concept of prosperity was wrong.

A Complete Idiot

The course was an eye-opener in other ways. I lived in something like a cell with five or six colleagues. Each of us had a bedroom with a bathroom but we shared a living room. I had arrived alone and was later joined by my wife and our first two children: our son Harri, who had been born in 1975, and our first daughter Maria, born in 1978. The psychologist spoke to my wife as well about the possibility of me becoming an entrepreneur.

'You'll need to support him,' he told her. 'Because this is another jump into the unknown.'

Kukka-Maaria had been the most immense support to me throughout my years of travelling. She was totally committed to me and believed completely in my success. She taught me a new way of living, educating me into the Western understanding of hard work and morality. She was my best friend as well as my wife.

In the early days I acquired what seemed to me to be an enormous debt by buying our first two-bedroom apartment, all 54 square metres of it. This debt kept me awake at night. As my salary increased so did the size of our apartments and the size of the loans needed to purchase them. Taxes are high in Finland and it is hard to pay off loans from a salary.

The psychologist's words gave us a great deal of food for thought. Maybe this was a way to make enough money to get out of debt and actually start to accrue some capital. But still I was very hesitant to do as he suggested. I felt I owed Mr Grotenfelt everything, and if I was unpopular with my colleagues now, how much more unpopular would I become if I insisted on making a move which was virtually unheard of in Finland, and which would almost certainly make me independently wealthy within a few years? On the other hand I liked the idea of being independent of the company, of escaping the envy and corporate infighting. I didn't have any ambition to become president of Tampella and I was beginning to think I

Fighting it Out

didn't have the strength for internal politics any more.

As I dithered, Kukka-Maaria was a rock.

'To hell with it,' she said. 'What's the worst they can do to you? Fire you? You're only thirty-five; you'll soon find another job.'

The course ended, we received our diplomas, had pictures taken and departed. Two days later I was back at work in our new headquarters in Helsinki, with a magnificent view overlooking the harbour. Mr Grotenfelt's secretary phoned down to invite me to the fifth floor with my diploma. I duly took it up and showed it to him. He grinned broadly and patted me on the back.

'Well done!' he said. 'Now, tell me what you've learnt because I have great plans for you.'

I explained how Harvard had given me a whole new way of looking at business, teaching me to analyse situations strategically and make decisions accordingly. I told him about the case studies of real companies that we had worked on, companies that were sick and needed turning round.

'I've also learnt this,' I said, feeling simultaneously proud, guilty and scared, 'but I don't think you're going to like it.'

I placed my resignation politely on his desk. He picked it up and read it, the colour rising in his cheeks. He grew redder and redder and although he opened his mouth to speak no words seemed to come out. After what seemed like an age he managed to regain his powers of speech.

'This will not happen! Did those bastard Americans tell you to do this?'

'Yes,' I replied, truthfully.

'It can't be. I'm also president of the Federation of Finnish Industry. The policy of all employers is not to allow employees (he used a word which also meant mercenaries and slaves) to get rich. If we make an exception for one, anyone else in a key position will want the same. You have to understand this. It's simply policy. We do not allow our employees to become brokers.'

I forced myself not to allow him to batter me into submission without a fight. 'My case is unique. You sent me to Russia and Japan! You yourself told me that if I succeeded the sky would be the limit. I could set up a company and continue doing exactly what I have been doing up to now. It would be better for you, too.'

The idea was too shocking for him to contemplate. There was nothing for me to do but go back downstairs, pack my things and go home. Nobody made any attempt to stop me. Once I got home I sat with Kukka-Maaria and we gloomily flicked through the newspapers in search of work. I couldn't take in the fact that everything I had worked for had disappeared so easily. When the phone rang it was Mr Grotenfelt's secretary.

'Mr Tilev,' she said, 'why aren't you at work? Come quickly, the president is looking for you.'

I abandoned the newspapers, leapt into the car and drove straight back. I went up to Mr Grotenfelt's office again. He stood up, towering over me, and held out his hand.

'I'd like to congratulate a future millionaire,' he said as we shook hands.

He was so determined to keep me that he negotiated with all the other big Finnish companies, who gnashed their teeth but eventually agreed to make me an exception to the rule.

So, at the beginning of 1983, I found myself the owner of a private company, in a market where I had no competition and the right to add any other products to my range that did not compete directly with Tamrock products. Concentrating mainly on metals and machinery I traded with Western Europe, Russia, America and Japan, but it was in Russia that I had the market to myself.

I didn't have to go out looking for new clients. Over the years I had been approached by any number of companies

Fighting it Out

asking if we would represent them in the Russian market. As soon as they heard what had happened they came banging on the door from as far afield as Germany, Britain, America and Italy. We were in the enviable position of having a virtual monopoly of the biggest market for mining equipment on earth. We had been one of the most successful sales organisations in the world for some time, now we were going to be one of the most profitable as well.

I only wanted to represent manufacturers of big capital equipment. I didn't want to be involved in the labour-intensive supply of nuts and bolts. But that still was a huge field. There are thousands of different machines needed in the mining process. Tamrock's machines were at the start of the process, but behind them were giant flotation factories, crushing factories and a hundred other expensive processes, billions of dollars worth of investment. I wanted to be able to do as big a volume of business as possible, employing as few people as possible. We contacted the end users of the equipment to find out who the best international manufacturers were and then agreed to represent them.

Many of the manufacturers were struggling to maintain a presence in the market from hotel rooms, just as I had once had to do. Having us represent them, with our infrastructure of offices, cars and secretaries and our tailor-made contacts, made perfect sense. Within months it was obvious that the company was going to be a colossus. Mr Grotenfelt was right; I was going to be a millionaire.

CHAPTER NINE

TREACHERY AFOOT

My being away at Harvard for six months had given some of my colleagues within Tampella the ideal opportunity to try to supplant me.

Although I have been lucky to have had many good and loyal friends, I have discovered in my life that friendship is a precarious business. There is often betrayal lurking behind it. One can only be betrayed by a friend; an enemy can never betray you. In the first six years I was with Tampella I had gone from being a complete nobody to being the third most senior man in the group. It would have been surprising if that had not aroused resentment in those around me. Some of them thought that once the joint manufacturing agreement was set up with Russia I was no longer needed. When I was out of the way in America they started to execute their plans for my removal.

One of the directors ordered that any contract, even for a single screw, should from now on be signed by anyone but me. He wanted to show that they could do without me. The first person he and his fellow plotters ran up against was the man who I had set up the joint venture with in Russia, a man who had become a personal friend. They promised him a free machine if he signed for them.

He was a tall elderly man, with grey hair and piercing blue

Fighting it Out

eyes. I can imagine how he looked at them as he asked. 'Where is Atanas?'

'He's in the States and won't be back for months.'

'Well, we're not in a hurry, are we? When he comes back, tell him to come and I'll sign.'

Next they went to the deputy minister of Mintransstroi, a cunning softly spoken Armenian. They tried to arrange a meeting.

'Tampella is a great company,' he told them, 'but we are greater still. And there is an equasion mark between us. Do you know what that is?'

The Finns were silent.

'It is Atanas,' he laughed, 'and until he comes back, don't even come to me. We have nothing to discuss without him.'

It was because of friendships like these, built over the years on mutual trust, that I was in such a strong position. These people had given me their word that they would deal with me, and that was enough. Furthermore, I was no stranger to plots being hatched behind my back. I had already been up against more dangerous men than my Tampella colleagues due to my connection with Dr Karjalainen.

At the end of 1980 President Kekkonen, who was eighty years old, became seriously ill. It was obvious to everyone that he would not be able to complete his term and there would have to be elections. My father-in-law was the most likely man to succeed him at the time. Despite his enormous popularity, he was not without rivals in his own party and the other parties. They immediately set to work to ensure he did not come to power.

One peaceful Sunday afternoon we were all at home. I was playing with my children in the living room when the doorbell went. I opened the door and was blinded by exploding flashbulbs. Spotlights glared into my eyes as television cameras turned and a forest of microphones surged forwards, pushing me, blinking, back into the house. There was a barrage of questions as everyone talked at once, but I couldn't make sense of what they were saying. I had no idea why they were there or what they wanted from me.

After a while they realised I couldn't answer their questions unless they explained to me what was happening and one of them held up the front page of a right-wing German newspaper, *Welt am Sonntag* for me to read. The headline was: THE LIVING MICROPHONE FOR THE KGB!

Beneath the headline was a picture of me and my family, and another of Dr Karjalainen and my wife. I snatched the paper and read it, ignoring the questions that continued to rain down on me. The story claimed I was an agent for the KGB and had been working as a spy in the heart of the Prime Minister's family. It was a story that would never have got into any Finnish paper, where all the editors knew me well and also knew they would be sued for printing such lies. The perpetrators had had to travel to Germany to find anyone who would believe such rubbish, let alone publish it. Now that the accusations were out, however, they became a story in themselves and I was caught up in the eye of a giant political storm that raged across the Finnish newspapers and television screens.

As soon as I could get out of the house, I went straight to Mr Grotenfelt, who I still worked for at that stage, and told him what was happening. He laughed.

'Don't worry, Atanas. They want to get your father-in-law, not you. It's a deliberate smear campaign.'

I was pleased he wasn't concerned, but I was also determined to put a stop to it. I told him I intended to sue Springer, the German publisher of *Welt am Sonntag*.

'How on earth are you going to sue Springer?' he asked. 'He's one of the biggest publishers in Europe. His lawyers will tear you to pieces.'

I refused to be pacified. All my instincts told me to do

Fighting it Out

whatever I could to save the name of my family, particularly my father-in-law. Against everyone's advice I flew to Hamburg and hired the best lawyers I could find. I started proceedings against the newspaper. In the midst of it all I still had to work, which meant travelling to the Soviet Union as usual. I told Mr Grotenfelt my problems.

'If I go, they'll say I'm receiving new instructions from the KGB, and if I don't go they'll say I'm scared because I'm guilty.'

He patted me on the shoulder. 'Just look after your own business and pay no attention to anything they might say,' he advised.

Grabbing my briefcase I went straight to the airport. I didn't need any more luggage because I had clothes and everything I needed at the apartment in Moscow. I was among the first passengers to get off the plane, and because I had a permanent visa I never usually had my bags opened, but that day they asked me to open my briefcase.

I had a copy of Welt am Sonntag in the case, with the headline and my picture clearly visible. The customs officer did not speak German, but he recognised the initials KGB and looked for a moment as if he was going to swallow his tongue.

'What is that?' he spluttered.

'Just an article,' I replied.

He called over an interpreter who read the piece through, the colour draining slowly from his face. Other Finns were peering curiously over my shoulder, trying to work out what was going on. I felt embarrassed. The situation was ridiculous but also disturbing. I had no idea how they were going to react. I decided to brazen it out. I pulled out my passport.

'Comrade Customs Officer,' I said. 'This is my passport. Can you see my name?'

He nodded.

'Do you see the same name in the newspaper story about the KGB?'

He nodded.

'Then you must draw your own conclusions,' I said, snapping the passport shut.

The man obviously decided it would be better not to get involved in secret matters and composed himself. His face lit up and he welcomed me to Moscow. For a few moments, it seemed, I had become a Soviet hero.

In Hamburg there were endless dirty dealings before we reached the courts, resulting in postponements and prolongations, but I refused to give up and eventually, because they couldn't produce one single shred of proof, I won. Springer was forced to publish an apology on the same page as the offending article had been and took back all the lies, as well as paying me financial compensation. I did the same with the Finnish television stations and newspapers who had talked and written about the case, forcing them to take their words back.

The lawyers dug deep and discovered that the whole smear campaign had originated in Finland, started by people who were scared of my father-in-law.

When I read in the papers in 1987 that a large private bank had bought Tampella, I thought little of it. The company, after all, was 170 years old, one of the biggest concerns in Finland and Scandinavia, with a long tradition of operating internationally. It had been founded by two expatriate Scotsmen who chose to build their futures in a beautiful spot beside a waterfall, between the two lakes of Tampere. The resulting company was a source of great pride for Finnish industry and part of its history, so it was surprising to read that such a venerable institution had fallen into the hands of a bank, but not alarming in any way.

'It will be good for us to have the backing of a bank,' the management explained to me, and I saw no reason to question their judgement at that stage. Perhaps if I had still been an

Fighting it Out

employee of the company I would have been more disquieted by the change of ownership, but by then I had my own business and felt that my contracts with Tampella were safe.

These were the casino years of the eighties and early nineties, when banks were spending money like water and there was economic extravagance everywhere in Western Europe and Japan. By pumping too much money into the economy by way of loans, the banks were creating a bubble of inflation. There was a compound around the emperor's palace in Tokyo, for instance, which at one time was worth more on paper than the whole of California.

This particular bank proved to be one of the most arrogant and aggressive of all Finnish banks. Its board of directors consisted of a group of close friends who may, or may not, have been good bankers, but who hadn't the slightest idea about industrial or commercial activities. They had come to power after the suicide of their boss, voting one another into positions of influence. They wanted to conquer the world with borrowed money and artificial liquidity, creating a huge, world-beating institution. They succeeded in destroying Tampella and the bank completely within five years of taking control.

Things went wrong almost from the first day. Although they had paid an enormous amount for Tampella, they made no effort to inform even the senior managers of the change of ownership. A few days later they fired all the directors. One of the more junior bankers then came to see me, and told me to increase the prices in the Russian market by 25 per cent.

'I'd like to raise them by two hundred per cent,' I said, 'but unfortunately it doesn't work like that.'

He didn't want to listen. He was brimming with self-confidence.

'I am ordering you to raise the prices by twenty-five per cent,' he said.

Treachery Afoot

By then I was already rich in my own right. I certainly didn't have to do what he told me.

'Good bye,' I said, showing him the door.

I knew what had happened, they'd gone through the books, seen how much profit I was making and decided to keep it for themselves. They'd misunderstood completely what the purpose of business was. Business is about creating something out of nothing and requires ideas and knowledge. Money is simply a by-product of doing it right. They thought they could put the money before the business, which meant they were doomed. I was saddened by what they were doing, but not really hurt. You can only be hurt by people you respect and care about.

Our relationship staggered on for another year but eventually the bankers forced Tampella to renege on our agreement. They violated the contract of representation, which led to arbitration and a legal settlement of the relationship. It was all over as quickly as that. Hundreds of millions of dollars a year, which had been coming into my company, stopped. If I wanted to continue on my road to wealth, I was going to have to change direction very fast indeed.

I was becoming increasingly disillusioned with the Finns, not only because of my own experience, but also partly because of what was happening to my father-in-law. After forty years at the top of the political tree the effort of protecting himself from the envy and aggression of those around him had begun to prove too much. He'd been Kekkonen's right-hand-man for thirty years, but towards the end of the president's life divisive people managed to drive a wedge between them and caused them to quarrel. Just before he died Kekkonen admitted he had been wrong to fall out with his friend, but it was too late; Dr Karjalainen's heart was broken. His world seemed to collapse around him. It was as if he had been betrayed by his own father.

Fighting it Out

Like all good Finns he didn't cry on other people's shoulders; he kept the pain inside. Although he remained a minister, he turned in on himself and started drinking heavily. He began to avoid coming home because the media were always camped out on the doorstep. He became an alcoholic and his marriage started to show signs of strain. The situation also put stress on my own marriage.

Until that moment I had never seen him ill for a moment, not even a runny nose, but drink was destroying him. It was like watching a man committing suicide, very slowly. We all tried to help him and he gave endless promises and then broke them, like all alcoholics. I persuaded him to go to a clinic in Switzerland, where one of the rules was that you must confess to your alcoholism in order to start fighting it, but he always referred to the trip as, 'When I was in Switzerland on holiday...' At the beginning of the eighties he lost the presidential election and finally fell into a spiritual abyss. He died in 1990.

The bankers who had taken over Tampella succeeded in destroying fifty billion dollars' worth of business within five years, half of which was Tampella itself. They were all fired and brought to trial, but the courts decided they had had no intent to lose the money and they walked free. How could anyone lose fifty billion dollars unintentionally?

My disillusionment with Finland was complete.

CHAPTER TEN

HIS ROYAL HIGHNESS, KING SIMEON II

During 1981 I had the pleasure of making the acquaintance of His Royal Highness King Simeon II in Switzerland. The many meetings and talks we have had have turned my initial warm regard for this extremely refined and intelligent man into lasting respect. Bulgaria missed an important opportunity in failing to find a way to use the influence and prestige of the King, especially during the incredibly tough period following the fall of Communism, in the years immediately after 1989.

There is no doubt in my mind that we would all have profited if our country's governments had shown more resourcefulness, good-will and imagination in making use of his international connections. His bearing and dignity would have been invaluable at that time in setting a standard for public life in Bulgaria, and this would have helped to calm the wild Balkan temperament as well as tame the so-called 'political élite'.

I had some interesting experiences with His Royal Highness between 1984 and 1985. At that time we invited him to visit the Tameplla concern and we welcomed him at the highest

Fighting it Out

state and company level. The President of Tampella asked the King to extend his help to our subsidiary companies and enterprises in different countries. He accepted and I can claim with pride that to this day many of my former colleagues remember the help and the wise advice they received from His Highness.

During the King's visit, he and I attended an important meeting at the National Bank of Finland. We had half an hour to spare beforehand and we decided to take a walk down one of the main streets in Helsinki. Everything was fine until it started raining. To escape the downpour, we entered the shop of a Serbian friend of mine by the name of Milan – a big joker. It was a large shop, but the quality of the goods was not of the best. I usually brought Russians on business trips and other such guests from the socialists countries to his shop to pick up bargains. I invited the King to have a laugh with this Serbian and to shelter from the rain.

At the entrance we were greeted by Milan himself, with a 'Hi, mate, what's up?' I introduced them without revealing the King's identity. Milan, laughing throughout and patting the King familiarly on the back, proceded with the hard sell. 'Come on my friend, chose a raincoat and I'll give you a 25 per cent discount.'

Some time later, when the King had left, I went to see Milan again. 'Do you know who that man was?' I asked. He did not, and when I explained, he was so surprised that his eyes nearly fell out of their sockets. But, like every Serbian, he recovered quickly and immediately started boasting: 'I knew he was a refined gentleman when he didn't react to my 25 per cent discount. But you never know, I said to myself. Business is business, after all.'

The King has been a good friend to me and always keen to support business. It was with the help of the King that I was introduced to the former and present Prime Minister of

His Royal Highness, King Simeon II

Morocco, who was at that time, for a short period, the head of the State Monopoly of Phosphates. His Highness had very close relations with the King of Morocco, where some of the largest phosphate deposits in the world can be found, and as a consultant for Tampella, he set up the meeting so that we could sell some of our mining machines. He was also present during the talks and helped us all the way through.

It is this mixture of regal role model and pragmatic businessman which makes King Simeon uniquely qualified now to lead Bulgaria out of the economic morass and towards a brighter future.

CHAPTER ELEVEN

KILLING MY BABY

There is a saying of Marcus Aurelius which is useful to remember whenever things look blackest: 'There is nothing that can bring you down unless you decide to let it. If you realise that it is outside you, and has no power over you, then nothing can kill you.' It's all a question of attitude. I wasn't about to give up several hundred million dollars of turnover a year just because a bunch of greenhorn bankers had messed up, but I was obviously going to have to make some serious strategic changes.

There are many books about business strategies and how to implement them. What they seldom tell you, however, is that there is no strategy that suits all businesses. Life is mobile, changing all the time, and business is just part of life. It's far better to have no strategy, otherwise you're bound by it and you exclude the alternatives. To be successful you have to be prepared to change all the time, constantly reversing and adapting previous plans, keeping your mind open and flexible. It's never a weakness to change your opinions according to the facts. Routine is bad for us because it kills our spirits and our souls, whereas change brings new opportunities and new

Fighting it Out

horizons. The Chinese character for change is the same as the one for possibility. As long as you have a vague goal, that is enough, and the road by which you get there is more important than the goal itself. The windier the road the more interesting the journey. Tactics, however, should be clear.

It was time for me to make some changes and come up with some new tactics. I met up with the former leadership of Tampella. We talked for hours before making a decision, and then phoned the senior management of Atlas Copco, one of the companies I had forced out of the Russian market when I took Tamrock in and formed the joint manufacturing deal. Atlas Copco was part of the gigantic Wallenberg concern, which owned 35 per cent of Swedish industry. Other companies under the same umbrella included Saab, Astra, Ericsson and Electrolux. Like Tamrock, the company was a world leader in equipment for mining, tunnelling and loading. My Finnish friends and I suggested we took charge of their branch in Moscow, a branch we had made redundant by taking all the market; thanks to me they hadn't sold so much as a button in the Soviet Union for fifteen years, although their equipment was almost identical.

Although the bosses in Sweden could see the sense in what we were suggesting, company policy didn't allow them to appoint people from competitors. We had a long series of discussions while they used their own channels of information to find out what was happening at Tampella.

'OK,' the boss finally said to me. 'We can see that what is happening at Tampella is madness, and that they seem to be willing to ruin their own monopoly, the one you spent fifteen years building for them. Here's what we propose: if you can arrange one deal for us within the Soviet Union, of any size at all, we'll appoint you our representative for five years.'

I caught the next plane to Moscow.

I met Ivan Vassilievitch Gloushkov, the deputy minister for

non-ferrous metallurgy in the USSR. We'd enjoyed a long working relationship and respected one another. I explained the situation to him and he called a meeting of all the people who had authority to purchase mining equipment. I explained what had happened again, and that Tampella seemed to be determined to cut off the branch it was sitting on.

'I believe you shouldn't worry about whether the Finns are making a mistake,' I said, 'even though their actions are harming you to a degree. What you should do is turn to Atlas Copco.'

'But we haven't seen hide nor hair of Atlas Copco for fifteen years,' they protested. 'We don't even know the brand names of their equipment. All our institutes of higher education teach everything about Tampella and Tamrock. You know that, Atanas; you set it all up. We don't have a comparison of prices. We have no references. For fifteen years we've been sending reports to Gosplan, telling them there's nothing better than Tamrock. Now you're asking us to turn round and claim the exact opposite? You want us to tell them we were lying to them, with the KGB watching?'

I couldn't think of anything to say. Everything they claimed was true. The situation was ridiculous. How could I ask them to do something I had been swearing for fifteen years they should not do? Then Gloushkov started to talk.

'We must change our ways,' he said. 'There's a new market economy now. We can't go on relying on a monopoly situation. It's 1988; perestroika is here to stay.'

After hours of going back and forth we found enough grounds to write a new report for Gosplan, suggesting they add Atlas Copco and some other competitors to the list of companies whose equipment they considered for every job. Three weeks later someone at Metalurgimport phoned and invited me in to sign a contract.

I called Magnus Unger, the president of Atlas Copco in

Fighting it Out

Stockholm. 'Would you like to come and sign a contract in Moscow?' I asked.

'I don't believe it. You've persuaded them? I've never been to Moscow, what should I do?'

'We'll take care of you,' I reassured him. 'We have cars, offices, everything you need. Just come.'

When he arrived we drove him to Metalurgimport, where the president of the organisation met him in person. There were other bosses from Mintsvetmet and we gathered round for the signing of the first contract for twenty five million dollars. Champagne corks were popping and the atmosphere was like one big party. It was the biggest single order for Atlas Copco in fifteen years. A week later I was in Stockholm to sign a contract that made me a representative of the company. From that day Tamrock never sold another thing in Russia. I had successfully killed my own baby, and the anger of the new management at Tampella knew no bounds. They obviously had not expected me to take them on; they certainly didn't expect me to win. They immediately wanted revenge.

Two of them used prominent relatives in the Finnish government to get in touch with the KGB and leak a false document claiming that two Russian contacts and I had supplied incorrect spare parts for the Tamrock machines. They claimed that by doing this we had damaged the Soviet mining industry and the whole economy of the USSR, because Tamrock machines were so heavily used.

The KGB immediately believed this ridiculous lie, without even bothering to check it. The whole repressive machinery of the empire swung into action and my Russian friends narrowly escaped being sent to concentration camps, a fate which was still quite common in Russia. Although I was safely outside the country at the time the scandal broke, it seemed likely I was going to be hurt too. I had gone from being accused of being a KGB spy to being accused of attempting to bring about the downfall of the Soviet Union. This time I was saved by history. The Soviet Union disintegrated at exactly the right moment.

Later it was revealed that the contact had been bribed by the Finns to spread the stories, and he was thrown out of the KGB. But, like many others, he had already succeeded in storing up enough money to survive in the post-communist world.

While I wholeheartedly welcomed the collapse of communism within the Soviet Union, it put an end to my business interests there. The monopoly I had enjoyed was ended when the mines were privatised and a full-scale gangster war erupted. For all its shortcomings, the Soviet system had been very free of corruption. Who could take bribes when the KGB was watching everyone? Even if someone had asked for a bribe, what would they have spent it on without drawing attention to themselves? Where could they have banked it? Likewise, there were never any problems with being paid. So many signatures and countersignatures were needed on every document that it was impossible to end up with a phoney contract, and everyone paid like clockwork. All those inhibitions vanished overnight and everyone started asking for bribes, from the lowest doorman to the highest politician.

Part of this new mafia was created by the former custodians of the state. When they saw that they had to dismantle the system, one way to survive was to create secret organisations that could use old connections for blackmailing and corruption. Those who had access to KGB files could now use the secrets for financial rather than political gain. Doing business became impossible in such a climate of chaos and distrust. It was time to look for new pastures.

It was in 1992, as I prepared to return to Bulgaria, that my wife and I agreed to part. Despite our long and successful marriage, Kukka-Maaria and I had drifted apart, after twenty-five years together and three wonderful children.

Fighting it Out

We all talk incessantly about love, since, like the sky, it is above everything. From the love of your homeland to the love of your children, from the love of your mother to the love of a woman, it is one of the most sacred of human feelings. But I believe the idea of marriage is a little antiquated. How can you vow to love the same person all your life when you are still in your early twenties? It's like filling out a blank cheque, without knowing the amount that will eventually be written onto it. How can you promise to love someone in thirty years' time when you have no idea how you both will look or how your personalities will have developed? People find new values and deny old ones; change their points of view, sometimes even their religious beliefs. It would be terrible if they didn't. Who wants to die exactly the same as they were born?

Historically there was sense in the marital institution. It was created to protect children and women at a time when they were entirely dependent on men financially and for their social status. Now, in the developed world, women are equal members of society and don't need this patronising protection. In the past they had to put up with treatment they did not deserve, simply to stop their men from abandoning them. They no longer have to do that. So I do not accept the inertia of the past and the dramatising of the divorce rate as some terrible horror. Artificially continuing a marriage turns family life into never-ending war. There is nothing bad, I believe, in a civilised separation, admitting that when we exchanged those vows a quarter of a century before, we were different people. That is, I believe, what happened to Kukka-Maaria and me.

Maybe we should introduce limited marriage licences, perhaps for ten years. Then, if everything is OK, you both sign up for another ten years at the end of the first decade. If you can't stand the sight of each other any more, then you go your own ways with no lies or vulgar dramas.

Nor does marriage seem necessary when two people are

truly in love. What does the signature of an indifferent clerk on a certificate of marriage mean to two people in love? People live together because they love and need each other, not because they've signed a piece of paper. Real love is unconstrained and doesn't tolerate forcefulness. The majesty of love lies in its unpredictability, in its lack of subordination to any laws, rules or terms. They call it blind because it doesn't take into consideration the generally accepted norms, least of all the boring formalities. It's selfless, without boundaries, and if you try to chain it up it dies immediately. Like art, it is spiritual, not material, and emanates straight from the heart. We should pity the man who has not loved, has not felt the freedom which love bestows upon you. Such a man has never lived.

I've been extremely lucky in love. I've loved my parents, friends and the few women I have shared different stages of my life with. When I have fallen in love each experience has been unique and wonderful, neither resembling nor replacing previous ones.

It's not by chance that love has always been a creative stimulus for great composers, writers and poets. It's indifferent to wealth or social status. It's the creation of God, while money is the devil's work. Love turns all of us into more generous and magnanimous creatures, helps us to widen our horizons.

Christianity links love with hope and belief because they're the essence of man. It's impossible to live your life meaningfully unless you believe, hope, love or are loved. If you believe in yourself, in the future, in virtue, you cannot but believe that your dreams will come true, that your bravest endeavours will one day bear fruit. You also hope that your children will grow up healthy and find their place in the world and that you will live a long and fruitful life, that your house will not fall apart, that a train will not run over you. You hope that humanity does not completely lose its mind and destroy itself. Hope is life's beam of light, the warm spot without which we're lost. It's not for no reason that we say hope dies last. For me, hope is also connected to the craving for love, which closes the circle and makes our presence on earth not only more tolerable, but also more meaningful.

CHAPTER TWELVE

DOWN AND OUT IN MILAN

No matter how well you do or how far you come in life, it's easy for it all to slip away. It's important to remember that wealth and power are just trappings and they can disappear overnight leaving us no different to anyone else walking the streets. This frightening truth was brought home to me one pleasant day in the early 1990s.

I was due to go to a castle in Geneva, where I had been involved in organising one of a series of exhibitions of young Bulgarian painters under the patronage of my friend King Simeon II of Bulgaria. Although I was the main organiser of the event I never actually got there, because for a few days I simply disappeared from sight. I officially ceased to exist.

I had spent the night before in Venice with a Bulgarian lady friend. That morning we'd set off early by car. When she discovered we were to be passing through Milan the lady started pestering me to stop so we could see the sights. I was already growing a little tired of her endless whims, and this one seemed particularly ridiculous.

'Milan?' I said. 'You must be joking. It's a big city. How can you see a city like that in passing? We'll come some other time.'

Fighting it Out

But she wouldn't give up her nagging and eventually I gave in.

'OK,' I conceded. 'You have half an hour.'

I stopped the car, a Mercedes 560SEL, in the middle of town, locked it and set off to see some sights. When we returned thirty minutes later the car had disappeared with all our clothes, documents and credit cards. I was standing in the middle of Milan in nothing but my denims and a shirt with three or four stray dollars in the pocket.

We went straight to the police and wrote reports, gave evidence and signed everything put in front of us. The policemen were laughing.

'A car like that you'll only ever see again in your dreams,' they told us. 'Nobody gives back such a souvenir.'

I sent the lady on to Rome, to the Bulgarian embassy, where she hoped to get help, a new passport and some means of returning home. I stayed in Milan. I, after all, was a Finnish citizen and would have to approach different people.

I decided the first step was to find some lodgings and went directly to Principe de Savoy, the finest hotel in the city and the one where I usually stayed. I greeted them cordially and told them my name.

'I've been robbed,' I said. 'I have no documents and no money, but I have been a guest here on many occasions.'

They consulted their computer and, of course, my name came up.

'OK,' the receptionist said, 'if you can just prove that this is you.'

'How can I prove it?'

'Could we see your passport?'

'What passport? That's what I'm trying to tell you. I was robbed of everything. If I had a passport, why would I be asking this favour?'

'OK.' They smiled serenely. 'Can you give us a credit card, then?'

Down and Out in Milan

It was like a scene from Kafka. We were talking to one another as if we were deaf, going in circles. I felt myself melting away, disappearing as a person, all my glory receding; the Mercedes which had seemed so secure just a few hours before, the money, the luxury, suddenly all that was left on the streets of the big city was an unidentified man with empty pockets. There was nothing the hotel receptionists could do to help me. For all they knew I was just some con man who'd come up with the name of Tilev and was trying to exploit it. I walked to the Finnish consulate and they promised to get to work on a new passport, but how would they get it to me? I told them I would contact them again once they had it. They told me I needed a photograph.

'Can you lend me some the money for a hotel?' I asked. 'I have nothing.'

They looked at me as if I was mad. 'How do we know who you are?' they asked. 'Every day all kinds of Finnish drunks come in here claiming they've lost something.'

'That's not the case with me,' I pleaded. 'At least lend me some money for photos.'

'We don't offer such services. You'll have to find the money elsewhere.' I could see they were entirely unmoved by my plight.

I wandered back out onto the streets and made my way to the station, where at least I knew there'd be somewhere to sit. I chatted to the drunks and bums for a while. Darkness was settling in and as it was too late to think about doing anything else, I resigned myself to an uncomfortable night on the benches. I didn't sleep much that night; most of the hours spent in surreal conversations with my fellow bums, and by the time morning arrived I felt very rough, and hungry. I wandered around the station, trying to loosen up my aching limbs and work out what to do. The shops were starting to open for the day's business. Spotting a children's clothes shop across from

Fighting it Out

the station I decided they were likely to be kind people. I told my new-found friends I would be back soon and walked across. Inside I found the owners, a pleasant young couple, and explained my predicament again. I offered to leave them my watch if I could just use their phone to make a few calls. To my immense relief they believed me. I had been beginning to think no one ever would again. I rang Kukka-Maaria and the children to tell them where I was and that I was safe. It felt strange to hear their voices, carrying on their normal lives while I was stuck in limbo. I didn't want to frighten them by telling them I was having to live on the streets. I also managed to make a call to my bank in Switzerland and explain what had happened to me, insisting they send me some money to get me out of the jam.

'Of course,' they said. 'Where shall we transfer the money to?'

I was trapped again. If I gave them an address to send the money to, I would still have to produce some sort of identification when I went to pick it up. But I had nothing to show. I explained again.

'Then there's nothing we can do,' they replied.

I was beginning to get angry. 'Then withdraw some money from my account and bring it down here personally.'

'How can we withdraw money?' They sounded genuinely confused. 'You're the only one who has access to your account.'

At that stage I lost my temper and told them it was their job to save me and to sort it out. A few minutes later they phoned me back at the shop and told me to wait and hope, because a taxi was coming from Zurich with the money. As if I had any other choice. They warned me that it would take a couple of days.

I returned to my friends on the station benches, who had not moved an inch since I'd been away, and slumped down among them. They asked how things were going and I explained my problem. It may have taken a while for the situation to sink through the clouds of alcohol fogging their minds, but as soon as it had they knew exactly what they had to do. They set about searching through every pocket and container they owned until they came up with enough change for me to be able to use the photo booth on the station. The picture that emerged was a shock. After a night without sleep and no razor, I looked like someone from a police dossier. I was starting to fit in on those benches; no one would have given me a second look.

After taking the picture to the Finnish consulate, I spent the next two days on the station, scrounging food and drink just like the other bums, waiting for the taxi to arrive from Zurich. It was a sobering experience; realising I only existed in the eyes of the world as long as I had papers to prove who I was. Money and possessions may just be symbols but it's hard to survive without them in the modern world. I could understand how the bums around me had reached the position they were in. It was very easy to lose control.

From a very young age I had understood that money was not part of who you are, because I had seen my family lose everything and still remain strong. Although it's pleasant to have wealth, not having it does not make you a worse person. My money was not actually part of my personality, not like the knowledge and culture I had soaked up over the years. It's only the development of the mind that makes a man different, and ultimately we ourselves and our children are our only real wealth.

Eventually the envelope arrived from Zurich, handed over by a banker who obviously had trouble recognising his esteemed client in his new disguise. I left my fellow bench-dwellers with enough money to ensure they still mention my name from time to time, and then went across to the little children's clothes shop to show my appreciation to the good people who had helped me.

'How much to buy everything?' I asked, pushing the money into their hands as they stared at me in disbelief. 'I wish you happiness and goodbye.'

The exhibition in the castle in Geneva, unfortunately, had to go on without me, but I had had a great deal of time to reflect on the meaning of riches and success. Just as money and success can be won, they can also be lost. It is always a mistake to judge a man by how many houses or cars he has; his real fortune lies in his nature, which comes to him by good luck but which he also has the opportunity to develop or destroy. He comes into the world with nothing else and he leaves with nothing else. It is good to be reminded of that now and again.

That wasn't the only time I regretted driving an expensive car. A few years later I was travelling around France in a Mercedes with my lady friend.

'Why don't we hop over to Barcelona?' I suggested. 'It's not too far away.'

We spent several days at a beautiful resort in the south of the city and then decided to go on to Madrid. As we drove we called the best hotels in the city to reserve a room, but found they were all full. The city, apparently, was hosting some major international event.

'Try the Ritz,' I told a tourist agent. 'I always stay there. They know me.'

But once again the word was the hotel was full.

'What about an apartment at the hotel?' I wanted to know. Still no joy.

'How much for the presidential suite?'

They named some astronomical price but by then I was desperate and accepted. We had about four hundred kilometres to travel, a lot of it through barren landscape. Arriving at the Ritz was like arriving in heaven. After a few days we set out once more to drive around the ancient capitals of Spain and on through Basque country to southern France. At the last traffic lights in town, where the great northern highway begins, we waited for the lights to change. At the green light I took off and three or four hundred metres further on I heard a rattling from the rear of the car. Something was knocking. I slowed down but the noise persisted.

A car drew level with us and a young boy called out through the window. 'You have a puncture.' I pulled over and climbed out. He was right. The back tyre was completely flat. The young Spaniard drew up beside us and got out. 'Let me help you,' he said with a broad smile. He had an open, honest face and I was grateful for his assistance.

We opened the trunk of the car and started to remove the luggage in order to get to the jack.

'You need to put that in the road, sixty metres away,' he said, handing me the emergency triangle.

Impressed with his conscientious approach to helping tourists in trouble, I did as he said. When I came back I rolled up my sleeves and started work with the jack, unscrewing the bolts and raising the wheel. My lady friend was watching me.

'Atanas,' she said, 'he's just run off.'

'What?' I straightened up in time to see the man's car disappearing in a cloud of dust. My attaché case, which had been on the car's small back seat and which contained all our documents, passports, money and credit cards, had gone.

Once I had changed the wheel we made our way back to the Ritz and they explained the scam to us.

'That's an old trick,' they said. 'The mafia hired professional psychologists to develop it. At the traffic lights they puncture your tyre from a distance, maybe with an airgun. Then they send a nice youngster to help you. It all happens in the light of day on a busy road, so you don't feel threatened. But there is another man in the youth's car, hiding, and while

Fighting it Out

you're distracted, moving luggage, putting out signs, opening your trunk, you lose sight of the car. The other one crawls out and steals whatever he finds. It just takes a few seconds.

'The criminals rely on using all the opposite things to those that would make you wary: light not darkness, an innocent-looking boy not a suspicious gang. Nothing would warn that you were about to be robbed.'

Things could have been worse; in all the fuss, I had left the keys in the ignition.

'We should have warned you,' the manager said apologetically. 'There's a whole mafia in Spain watching for foreigners like you, with expensive cars and a lot of money. They follow you from the border. Thank providence you didn't notice them or they could have stabbed you or shot you dead! So, consider yourselves lucky.'

It could have been a repeat of the Milan saga, but luckily the Ritz were willing to take us back in while we waited for everything to be replaced. Since then, however, I have not travelled in a beautiful car south of the Alps and, if I do, then I leave it in the hotel car park and take a taxi to go sightseeing.

These sorts of robberies are irritations and make you feel vulnerable for a while, but they're only petty criminals compared to the sort of people I have come up against in the business world, many of them in top positions. They are the real criminals milking the system of billions of dollars every day without ever having to operate a street scam or steal a car. They are the ones who are a real danger to society. They are the ones who have destroyed my home country.

CHAPTER THIRTEEN

MEANWHILE, BACK IN BULGARIA

Stara Zagora used to have its own opera, which was almost as famous as Sofia's. One evening in the early 1950s, squashed between my grandfather and grandmother, I heard one of the world's greatest tenors, the Bulgarian, Todor Mazarov, who was also from Stara Zagora. When he had finished singing, and the thunderous applause had died away, I was astonished to hear him thanking the audience in Italian. It seemed incredible to me that anyone could forget their mother tongue and I swore to myself that if ever I were to leave Bulgaria, I would never forget my roots. But by 1990 I could feel that my grasp of Bulgarian was weakening, some words escaping me completely. My mother tongue was disappearing into the past, like Church Slavonic.

I had spoken Bulgarian during my education, but even then it was poorer and weaker than it should have been, crowded with clichés and phrases I wouldn't use later. Over the years I have tried to evolve and enrich it by reading Bulgarian authors, but it still sometimes feels as if I'm still talking as I did when I was a small child. But however rusty the words might have become, the pull of my motherland never slackened. Memories

Fighting it Out

of my childhood have always remained vivid enough to bring tears to my eyes.

My country's authorities did not always have such fond memories of me. Before the start of *perestroika*, sometime in 1985, they branded people like me traitors, runaways and renegades, even though I'd left the country absolutely legally. *Perestroika* cleared the air, bringing fresher breezes through the stale halls of government and I, along with Koicho Belchev, decided that now we might be allowed to do something useful for our country. Koicho was an elderly fellow Bulgarian who had lived for many years in Switzerland and had wide and influential connections all over the world.

We thought about starting businesses in Bulgaria, to try to provide jobs and some income, but at that stage the country was too poor and sinking still further; so we decided to promote the country's artists, arranging exhibitions for young Bulgarian painters in different European countries.

I had always been attracted to the work of our classical painters, believing that a fine painting talks directly to a man's soul, and I have a wonderful collection of works by, among others, Bencho Obreshkov. I bought my Obreshkov collection in Vienna from an old woman whose husband was once a fellow student of the painter. Most of the paintings the family had received as gifts from Obreshkov himself.

It took me a long time to convince the lady that I was emotionally attached to these paintings and that if she would let me be the custodian of them, I would never break up the collection. I found these pictures helped me to deal with the longings which I still had for my homeland.

In my years travelling the world I have been able to visit all the greatest galleries, museums and private collections and I understand art not as a collection of single works but as a development of the human soul, a process unfolding through the centuries.

Meanwhile, Back in Bulgaria

In the Bulgaria that I went back to at the beginning of the nineties, I found little sign of any progress from the days when the communists first crushed everyone with any talent or education. The bitter truth is that Bulgaria still had no élite nor has one yet. For a while there was a newspaper called High Life, but its pages were full of closely shaven mobsters wearing sweatshirts and sporting gold chains around their necks and rings on their fingers.

The whole country was now so primitive there was no one to respect. An élite has to evolve in any society; it cannot be invented overnight. So there is little hope that things will improve quickly, but when communism crumbled at the beginning of the nineties, I still wanted to play my part in the renaissance of my homeland.

Blame for the sad state of Bulgaria cannot be laid entirely at the feet of the communists; five hundred years of Turkish rule also had a major influence on the area. But even that is not the whole story. It seems that we, the Bulgarians, have never wanted to live by the rules of God and man, to be part of the European family. We have always tried to have our cake and eat it and as a result we have a reputation as thieves, liars, murderers and charlatans. We assumed the role of a nation cleverer than its neighbours, a nation of great con men, always looking for the easy way out and never finding it.

In 1989 Zhivkov fell from power and negotiations began in Bulgaria for free elections. I, along with most of the people of my homeland, felt a surge of optimism. Laws of restitution were brought in and everything that had been confiscated fifty years before by the communists now had to be returned to its rightful owners. It was an incredibly difficult process, made harder by the fact that most people had never thought this day would come and had destroyed documents, proving what they rightfully owned. But it was definitely a start; maybe now, after years of suppression, we would finally be free to create a country we could be proud of. I believed Bulgaria was a youthful country again, ready for rebuilding and full of financial opportunities; another white spot on the world map for me to conquer.

What none of us knew was that the former communist leaders and their cadres had no intention of relinquishing power. Zhivkov was replaced by Andrei Lukanov and Alexander Lillov, the two great men of the Socialist Party. Lillov had been the right-hand man of Zhivkov and became chairman of the Bulgarian Socialist Party in 1989. Lukanov, who became Prime Minister in 1990, was a gifted and clever man and he could see that with President Gorbachev retreating in Russia the days of unlimited power were now numbered, but for a while the old guard still held all the reins. Along with his fellow ministers, Lukanov secretly devised a plan to systematically strip the country of all its wealth. They'd seen an opportunity to turn capitalism to their advantage, to transform political power into economic power. Communist theories might have been discredited, but as long as the same people held power they had the ability to rob the country cold-bloodedly of every scrap of wealth that was left. How right they were to see the writing on the wall was proved in 1991, when the people of Bulgaria finally had enough of deteriorating living standards. They stormed the mighty communist headquarters and set light to it. Lukanov and Lillov resigned, fearful that they would be executed, and an election was held.

When the Union of Democratic Forces (UDF) won the election it seemed like a victory for democracy, but it was still the same people working under a different guise. In order to give the impression there was a credible opposition the ruling party had simply split itself in two: the Red Party (the Bulgarian Socialist Party) and the Blue Party (the UDF). They

Meanwhile, Back in Bulgaria

then put themselves up for election. But whichever of them won, it would still be the same people in power, running both the government and the opposition. The fall of the government and the apparent change of power did not make any difference to their grand plan for robbing the country and making themselves some of the richest individuals in the world.

The collapse of communism in Bulgaria was no more than puppet theatre: positions were given to worthy professors and the like, but they were all still controlled by Lukanov and his cronies. There was no dissent, no protests in the streets; everything was planned by the people in power, who now called themselves 'new democratic forces'. And, all the time, they were putting their people in place in the country's banks and inventing companies in preparation for the great robbery. What could have been more tempting for them to exploit than a Bulgarian who had made a fortune outside the country and now wanted to return home to help rebuild his country? They started to lay a trap for me.

CHAPTER FOURTEEN

THE GREAT NATIONAL ROBBERY

It was not until 1996, that I finally reached the safety of Vienna, in the dramatic circumstances described in the beginning of this book. Leaving the dangers of my homeland behind once more, I felt a childish sense of excitement at having survived the whole adventure. I had lived through some dramatic and shocking experiences in the intevening years spent in Bulgaria, but the adrenalin-induced euphoria that washed over me following my escape was soon replaced by a deep sadness. I was going to have to accept that my hopes of helping my fellow countrymen had indeed been dashed. I might have had the satisfaction of outwitting the people who had tried to destroy me, but that didn't help those who were unable to escape and who were going to have to continue living in a country that had been impoverished all over again. I might have been able to obstruct the criminals' plans to enrich themselves as much as they had hoped, but I had not been able to stop them from bringing yet more ruin to the people they were supposed to be leading.

Two days after I got back to Vienna I received a phone call

Fighting it Out

from my lady friend, who was still in Sofia. She told me in a shocked voice:

'They've killed Andrei Lukanov.'

'What do you mean, killed him?'

'They've shot him in cold blood, on his own doorstep.'

I couldn't believe what I was hearing. I had been with Lukanov the night before I had escaped. He had indeed told me he was frightened they would try to get him but I hadn't taken him seriously. He had been one of them, the architect of the whole plan before it had spun out of his control, and now he was dead. It was an execution, ordered to frighten the opposition. It would paralyse the whole country and show everyone they were being ruled by gangsters.

'He was walking from his house to his car,' my lady friend went on. 'There was a mute tramp who had been rummaging around in the trash for a few days. He just ran across the road and opened fire.'

For me this was the final straw. Already a few days before, my guards had found two grenades set up as a booby trap behind the wall of my house. When the police came to remove them they had confirmed that the trap was, indeed, live and it was sheer luck no one had been hurt. The death of Lukanov, following so closely on my own narrow escape, finally I decided that night that my daughter, Maria, would have to be got out of Bulgaria immediately. I rang the house and spoke to Maria. I told her she had to get on the first plane out of Bulgaria, no more arguments. I spoke to the bodyguards and told them to make sure she did. If they were willing to murder Lukanov, a former prime minister and the original architect of their crime, in broad daylight, there was nothing they wouldn't be willing to do in their desperate attempts to complete their planned robbery.

When I had first decided to go back to Bulgaria at the beginning of the nineties I phoned Mr Grotenfelt, my former boss at Tampella, who was by then retired and was on holiday in Switzerland with his wife. I told him of my plans to return and take a role in the rebuilding of the Bulgarian economy.

'My children have grown up now,' I explained. 'Things are going well for me and I want to put something back into my homeland. I'm tired of living abroad and I want to contribute my wealth, my experience, my knowledge and my contacts to my country.'

'I take my hat off to you,' he said, having listened to me in silence, 'but if you think you'll find anybody happy to see you back, or if you think anyone will be interested in listening to your opinions, then you're fooling yourself.'

I was puzzled by his words but he went on to explain that he believed my countrymen would resent someone they saw as a traitor coming back to tell them how to do things. He said they'd try to steal from me and then they'd get rid of me. I chose not to believe his dire predictions. I'd waited two years after the elections, aware that the communists wouldn't disappear overnight, but I felt it was now safe to return, especially since the communist headquarters, that symbolic, grey, Stalinist structure, had been destroyed.

When I went back into the country to invest and rebuild, I had hoped that it would be possible to modernise and reform a former communist state overnight; it was not. The nature of communism is like that of a bird of prey, a predator looking only to tear things apart, rob and destroy. There may have been people with altruistic dreams at the start, but the people who actually rise to the top of the communist system are almost always venal, corrupt and mediocre. If they're given long enough to become entrenched in power they're impossible to remove, because all they do is reinvent themselves as 'democrats' and 'capitalists' – it's the same wolves, simply dressing themselves as lambs in order to continue their terrible work.

But in 1991 I had still been full of optimism as I watched the country take its first faltering steps towards democracy. It coincided with a time when I was thinking long and hard about what I wanted to do with the next part of my life. At that point I talked about it a great deal with my children. I had a strong feeling that emigration is not the best thing that can happen to a man. Back in 1971 I don't believe I had any alternative; now Bulgaria was in a terrible state and my opportunities to succeed lay outside, in a free market economy. I felt suddenly overwhelmed with patriotism. I also felt very disillusioned about the Finns, blaming them for my negative experiences at Tampella and for the ugly behaviour of the political opponents of my father-in-law. Perhaps the same would have happened in any country, perhaps it was just human nature, but to me it seemed to be personal to the Finnish people.

I wasn't so naïve as not to be aware that it would take a long time to turn Bulgaria round after such a disastrous half century, but I felt that if people like me didn't make a start on the task there was little hope Bulgaria would ever be able to move forward and take its place in a modern Europe as an orderly, calm and prosperous country. I was perhaps the wealthiest Bulgarian in the world by then; I felt that meant I had an obligation to put as much back into my land of origin as possible, both in the form of capital and business expertise. If I had thought too much about the potential problems I would never have done it, so I had closed my eyes and boarded a plane to Sofia, like a lamb to the slaughter.

Over the years I had maintained contact with many of my old school friends. The years between thirteen and eighteen are the most important in our development, and the friendships that you form during those years remain with you for ever, even if these friends go on to follow hugely different paths through life. When I saw those people again now, successful ministers or party officials, we still had a bond, although we were very conscious of our differences. When I asked them why they'd followed the paths they had, they explained there'd been no other way to prosper. They were all former members of the Communist Party, but they had never been believers in their hearts. That was why communism had evaporated so fast – there really was hardly anyone who felt strongly enough to fight for it.

I started my return to Bulgaria by forming a small company, putting a young man in charge whose father I owed a favour to. I needed a foothold from which to move forward. Old friends and relatives were the only people in the country I knew and trusted; I had to employ them, even if they weren't always qualified for the jobs I needed doing. I made some big mistakes and I would never normally hire people on those grounds, but in a primitive market like Bulgaria was back then, you have to revert to hiring people you know.

Normally, when I am recruiting I have very strict ideas of what I want. The most important quality is always intelligence, something that a person either has or doesn't have. Next comes personality, which has to be right for the job, but also tough and disciplined. Employees need to be honest and reliable if they are going to be of any use. Next comes education, which becomes more important as the world becomes more and more fragmented and specialised, and companies need people with specific skills. For senior people vision is also important, and finally, of course, experience. None of these criteria were relevant in Bulgaria at the time. There I needed people I could trust. Anything else was a bonus.

I wanted to own a bank, as it would provide a suitable instrument for the implementation of my plans, and I started looking around at the possibilities. I soon came across a new bank being set up, expressed an interest and became one of the founders and shareholders of the Bank of Agricultural Credit (BAC). The other main shareholders were the State Savings Bank (SSB), the State Insurance Institute (SII), Robert

Fighting it Out

Maxwell, who had 23 per cent and the Raiffeisenbank in Vienna, with 10 per cent.

Maxwell was a bully by nature, overbearing and arrogant, and had had a long-standing relationship with the communist bosses of the country, including a close friendship with Andrei Lukanov. He tried to use his position to take a leading role in BAC. I owned 10 per cent to start with and participated on the supervisory council without significantly interfering with the operational work of the bank. I was, after all, new to the business and needed to find my way. When Maxwell died in 1993, falling mysteriously from his yacht, Raiffeisenbank acquired his shares, making them the biggest shareholder with 33 per cent.

The day-to-day running of BAC was left to Yanko Yannev, a manager we all trusted implicitly. BAC became the biggest shareholder in the Dobrudjanska Bank in the town of Dobrich, which was in the process of developing into one of the best provincial banks in the country and was even accredited by a solid rating from the World Bank. Without realising it, I had stepped into the middle of a web of intrigue and become inadvertently involved in a crime so complex it is almost impossible for outsiders to comprehend.

With the bank set up and running, however, I still didn't have enough to fill my time. Since I knew so little about banking I looked around for other companies I might buy that I could take a more active role in, leaving the bank to take care of itself. It was to prove itself a time bomb ticking away in the background of my life.

During this whole period of the early 90s I was investing millions of dollars, feeling ridiculously optimistic about the future and prosperity of my country and its people. I founded an insurance and reinsurance company called Vitosha that quickly became one of the biggest and most stable in the country. I became the owner of Kontinent, a serious, new-conservative newspaper. This was a less impressive investment; it seemed the paper had no talent on the payroll whatsoever. The dead hand of communist propaganda had killed off any sparks that might have set the pages alight. Journalists were too used to printing the party line and never questioned anything the authorities did or said. There seemed to be no desire to work anywhere in the operation. After years of living under communist rule the lack of a need to fight for your daily bread kills something in the spirit of people. If you're going to be paid anyway, why make any effort? Those who had been running the paper for years were siphoning off any advertising revenue that came in via their extended families.

I had always believed that if I had shares in a newspaper it should be independent, above any political party, impartial and not influenced in its opinions by me. I made it a rule never to interfere in the day-to-day operations and never instructed the editors whom or what they could or couldn't write about. I discussed the general direction of the paper with the creative team and left them to get on with it. It's always been my belief that you should hire people who can do the job you want them to do, and then leave them alone to get on with it. All the people who run my companies have strict instructions not to bother me with mundane decisions, only to contact me with matters of substantial importance. I am still convinced this is the right policy in most situations. Delegation is a great art and the simple truth is that you cannot be everywhere at the same time. Some bosses try to make all the decisions themselves, but only a few geniuses can get away with that. Each of my companies has a separate management. We meet a few times a year to talk about our strategic and financial aims and then I leave them to it. If I feel I have to meddle then I should fire them and start again. A good company is like an orchestra. Every tone must be right, not almost right, but actually right.

Fighting it Out

My task is to be a good conductor, not to sing or play an instrument myself.

With Kontinent this approach was completely wrong. I was handing control to people who were totally unconscientious about their work. Furthermore, they seemed not to have built up any assets; there were no photo laboratories, computers, not even a car fleet. I might as well have opened the doors to a blast furnace and hurled several million dollars into it. Somehow, perhaps due to the lack of competition, it retained its image as a serious newspaper, but that was all. I had harboured great ambitions, and that made me vulnerable. When the newspaper's management tried to persuade me to buy them a printing house I almost agreed. Luckily, I was beginning to see the light and stopped myself wasting any more money just in time.

In my rose-tinted euphoria about my future in Bulgaria, I also set to work building myself a new home. Having been away from the country for so long I had nowhere to base myself. I was used to having a home in every country I worked in, complete with a wardrobe full of clothes and I could hardly move back in with my parents after so many years. I had grand plans. This would be the biggest and finest of my homes, because now I was back to stay. I wanted to use Bulgarian craftsmen, but I had forgotten just how unreliable and dishonest they all were. I found a great part of my time was spent being a foreman at the building site, just making sure they turned up for work and didn't steal anything.

Their incompetence seemed to know no bounds. All through the building process I had had a nagging suspicion that something important had been overlooked. Exactly what it was came to me one night when I woke with a blinding revelation: there were no chimneys! The idiots had built me a house with no way for the smoke to escape from the fireplaces!

Eventually, I had what must have been the finest modern villa in the country, complete with tennis courts, Italian bathrooms and beautiful art and furniture from all over the world. The house stands in a walled compound, with another smaller house for the security staff in the grounds. I felt I was putting down roots at last.

When corruption has entered into the soul of a people it is almost impossible to get it out; even the Church has become part of the communist rot. While on a camping trip with my son some years before, I had met the father superior of Rilla monastery. In 1994 I revisited the holy cloister. The father superior himself answered the door to my ring.
'God sends you, my child,' he said, not even waiting for me to kiss his hand.
'Why, Your Holiness?' I asked. 'What has happened?'
Ushering me in he told me a gloomy tale of how they had run out of money and signed a contract for economic maintenance and collaboration with a company which they had just discovered was owned by Turks. 'I would rather jump onto the rocks than allow the Turks to take this monastery!' he wailed.
I convinced him not to jump off the cliff yet, not until I had had my lawyers see what they could do to help. It didn't take them long to find a way out of the contract with the Turks' puppet company, and we entered into a new contract for the establishment of a joint company with 60 per cent owned by the monastery and 40 per cent by us. The company would be responsible for the monastery property outside its walls. The situation around the monastery at that time was terrible, a vista of stalls, tents and shelters swimming in dirt and effluvia. It looked like a flea market from the middle of the previous century. We set to work immediately, clearing the tin roofs and the stalls which spat burning oil from meatballs twenty-four hours a day. We built shops, two restaurants and two hotels,

Fighting it Out

designing them in an austere style to fit in with the atmosphere of the monastery, although they were still luxurious by Bulgarian standards.

The results were immediate, with the hotels filling up during Easter, Christmas and other religious and social holidays.

We revived the tradition of trading alcohol and wines, receiving international recognition, and constructed a branch of the bank close to the monastery, providing a range of services for tourists. Land that had been lying idle for decades was cultivated and made to bloom again.

I felt proud of myself for what had been achieved, like one of the great religious patrons of the past. I should have known better. The Bulgarian diseases of complaining and ingratitude soon raised their heads. The holy fathers decided that because I had left the country I must have gone into liquidation. Forgetting what a state they were in on the day I turned up on their doorstep, they started to attack me and other members of the company. They forgot the enormous sums of money we had invested in the area and wanted to keep every penny that came in, ignoring the debts that had been incurred and needed to be serviced. They wanted huge sums of money immediately. This drove the company into liquidation. It seems that religious people are no less greedy for earthly benefits than normal crooks. I could forgive the clergy their lack of economic experience, but not their greed.

At the bank the time bomb was ticking away. In early 1994 the Austrians from Raiffeisenbank had already begun to express suspicions about the chairman of BAC, Yanko Yannev. In order to take a closer look at the daily running of the operation they gained the right to include representatives in the management, which meant they could check all the credits and loans going out. They brought in a Bulgarian from America

The Great National Robbery

and some of their own people from Vienna. Even then, it would take them a year to discover what was going on; that BAC had over-extended itself in dubious loans without colateral. All of this had been set up by Yannev. He handed these loans over to his friends in a company that has come to be known as the Orion Group.

The group itself is an abstraction; it is not registered anywhere and it has no directors. It was discovered by chance by a journalist who was investigating a number of companies, all of which were being given enormous loans by different banks. It so happened that the journalist was also an astronomer and he noticed that all these companies, which appeared to have no connection to one another, had the names of stars in the Orion constellation. The name stuck. The companies receiving the money from the banks were each run by different people, but all those people were connected to the cronies who had surrounded Lukanov in his final days of formal power. Encompassing a wide range of diverse businesses, the Orion Group was nothing less than a front for the Bulgarian 'mafia' which had grown out of the government, made up of former secret service officers, ministers, arms dealers, spies and crooks.

Even before any of this puzzle started to make sense to us, the Austrians announced they wished to withdraw from BAC and start a new bank. They told me Yannev was not a respectable banker and had already ruined the bank. In my innocence I chose not to believe them. How could anyone believe such a far-fetched notion? Yannev was a well known banker, how was it possible that he was defrauding BAC? I thought that as a Bulgarian myself I would stand a better chance of getting to the bottom of what was going on than the Austrians.

Yannev and his friends came to see me. They convinced me the departure of the Austrians was the best thing that could happen to BAC and that we had to allow it; they played a nationalist card and persuaded me that we, as Bulgarians, could do this better without these foreigners. I normally have a golden rule that I never go into a business I know nothing about. For whatever fine motives, I had been breaking my own rules and I now made the worst mistake ever: I allowed myself to be convinced by their arguments.

The Austrians withdrew and I bought their shares, making myself the chief shareholder in BAC, owning more than 50 per cent. I was a banker with no experience in the business whatsoever, surrounded by people who had spent several years setting up a scam with roots that went so deep it was impossible to see them from the surface. It was a recipe for disaster but I was too far in to even contemplate backing out at that stage.

I can't say that I mourned Maxwell's departure from the scene in 1993. I did, however, feel very sorry for his sons, Kevin and Ian, particularly Kevin who I thought was extremely bright. I felt they had been bullied by their father when he was alive, just like everyone else, and had been left to face the music. I gave Ian a job on my newspaper and paid both of them fees for 'advising' me. I spent quite a bit of time with them both, including going to Annabel's, the most exclusive nightclub in London, where Kevin told me I'd better pay the bill since he and Ian were supposed not to have any money.

Soon afterwards they came to me with a partner, a polo-playing Canadian, and asked me to invest in a new joint project in the telecommunications business, which indeed I did, with close to a million dollars, representing 32 per cent of the Cyprus based company, SIC-TDS. When I realised I'd heard nothing about the investment, not even that it had gone wrong, I contacted Kevin. I teased him by recounting one of Aesop's fables. In this fable there is a snake that wants to get across a river, but can't swim. When a turtle comes along the snake begs for a lift across the water on his back. The turtle generously obliges, but when they reach the other side the snake gives his benefactor a poisonous bite. As the turtle lies dying he asks the snake why he would do such a thing.

'Because it's my nature,' the snake replied.

Did Kevin blush? Anyway, he assured me that my money was quite safe and would one day be returned to me with interest.

With the Austrians gone it was not long before I realised they had been right. Having been forced to take an interest in the management and having conducted several checks, I realised the truth. Yannev, through his wife and daughter, was involved in two companies in the Orion Group. I discovered he had OK'd unsecured loans of around seventy million dollars to those same companies. The money had been drawn out by a number of 'businessmen'; coarse men with low foreheads and low intelligence who seemed to wander in and out of the bank at will, demanding money which was passed on to various other companies within the Orion Group. The bank had been giving them whatever they asked for without asking any questions.

I also discovered that, among these friends of Yannev's, the bank had loaned ten million dollars to a man called Rumen Spassov. This was a name that struck fear into the hearts of anyone in Bulgaria who knew anything about the years of communist repression. His father, Mircho Spassov, had been the man most responsible for murdering the intelligentsia of the country. As a close adviser of Todor Zhivkov, and as Deputy Minister of Home Affairs, Mircho Spassov established infamous concentration camps in Belene, Skravna, Bogdanov Doll and Lovetch. In 1974 he was moved to the Central Committee and made chief of the military department, supervising the army and security, a department bigger than any ministry, putting him above all ministers. Due to the crimes and abuses at the camps

Fighting it Out

he was removed from his post in 1982.

The son was as bad as the father, but did not have the same political power. Instead he was using his influence to make sure he had a fortune stashed away outside the country. Rumen Spassov was at the head of the Orion Group, the grand master behind all that it did. It would be wrong to judge a man simply on the crimes of his father, but all enquiries into Spassov's character came back with evidence that he was a vicious, self-indulgent crook. I found that one of my secretaries had been to school with him, and she confirmed that even as a boy he had been stupid, a thief and a bully.

It became obvious to me that despite my lack of experience in the area, I would have to take over the operations of the bank in order to find out exactly what was going on and put a stop to it. However, I still didn't realise the size of the enemy I was coming up against. In 1994 we changed the two-level system of having a supervisory council and a board of directors to simply having a board of directors, with me as chairman and executive director. I had long serious conversations with Yannev. Although by now I was certain my suspicions were well founded, there was no action I could sensibly take; if I were to fire him I would be immediately severing all the channels for recovery of the missing funds. I explained to him I had no ambition to be a banker and that he would be my first deputy, with the same authority as before on one condition.

'I'm willing to let you keep all the honours and rights of your job,' I told him in front of the whole board, 'but the stolen money must be returned.'

My aim was to recover as much of the debt as possible and roll the rest of it over, but the total kept rising. Whenever I mentioned the Orion Group, Yannev would say the same thing: 'Leave them alone. They're dangerous people. They killed an architect only because the building he designed was not very stable on one side. They would think nothing of

The Great National Robbery

killing you.' But still he solemnly promised that Spassov would return the money he and his wife had been lent (between them they had 'borrowed' about forty million dollars from us), as also would a man called Slavchev who was the owner of a company called Agropromstroi, to whom Yannev had given forty million German Marks without any collateral. Slavchev was typical of the sort of puppets the communists had elevated to positions of influence because of their willingness to do as they were told and their inability to think for themselves. The Spassovs were using the money for their personal benefit and were transferring it out of the country, with plans to move to South Africa. They also used some of the stolen money to found a bank, which they called the Bulgarian Industrial and Agricultural Bank (BIAB).

Despite our differences, Yannev and I continued to work together, having daily meetings at one of which he told me that Jan Videnov, the leader of the opposition at the time, wanted to see me. The meeting was to be at the house of Lubomir Kolarov, later a minister of the neo-communist government and an active member of Spassov's Orion Group. I agreed to go.

At around two in the afternoon one day towards the end of 1994 I walked into Kolarov's house to find myself face to face with Spassov. Jan Videnov, a callow young man in his early thirties, arrived soon after me and Spassov immediately launched into a monologue, with Kolarov chipping in every now and then. The essence of the speech was that he had read in the papers about how I had taken over the running of the bank and was insisting that he and his wife returned the millions of dollars they'd borrowed.

'Would it not be better for you to write this debt off?' he enquired sweetly, 'because it's money needed by the party.'

'What party?' I enquired innocently. 'Are you planning to buy one?'

They went on to explain that I should forget the money

Fighting it Out

completely; making it clear they needed it to back Jan Videnov's Bulgarian Socialist Party.

'But it's not my money to give you,' I pointed out. 'I'm merely the banker. The money comes from the deposits of citizens and companies and I'm obliged by law to keep it safe. There's no question but that you must return the money. I cannot betray the trust of the people and shareholders who have voted me into this position.'

I noticed that Videnov remained silent through most of the discussion and was nodding approvingly at his cronies' arguments. In the end he grunted that it would be better if we could find a solution to the problem, but it was impossible. I was adamant I wanted the money; they were adamant they weren't going to pay it. It was probably at that moment that the death sentence on BAC was passed, although it would be some years before the execution actually happened.

The whole idea of people not honouring their debts was anathema to me. If I have one abiding rule of business it is that a man's word must be reliable. You should never deceive your business partners or customers and you should always pay your dues on the day and the hour that you contract to do so. That way people will keep on dealing with you. In my long and wide experience I remain convinced that the majority of the world is honest and I found this tacit acceptance of dishonesty in my own country bewildering.

Then, in an election in December 1994, the communists – in the guise of the Bulgarian Socialist Party – returned to power with an absolute majority, led by Jan Videnov, the young man who had been happy to sit there and sanction the stealing of the people's money by his cronies. There could have been no greater political disaster for Bulgaria. If things had been bad under Lukanov, they were about to become a great deal worse. We were plunging back into the Dark Ages after seeing no more than a tempting glimpse of the light at the end of the tunnel.

Despite the evidence of history, the Bulgarian people had chosen to believe the promises of the communists once more. They had chosen to believe the promise of bread at fifteen stotinki a loaf, and stories about how bright the future would be if they just avoided the clutches of the capitalist exploiters. I can only think they believed the lies because of their lack of experience of the market economy and their unclear understanding of the rules of democracy. It would be another two years before they finally saw the truth and by then untold damage had been done to the country, because this was communism with no other purpose than the plundering of a nation.

For a while I too tried to convince myself that things were not as bad as they seemed. Surely these people had the seeds of European socialism within them and had come to power with the intention of halting the destruction and proving that their party had some intellectual potential. I was fooling myself once more, and for that I would pay dearly.

After the meeting with Spassov I changed my approach in my role as chairman. From being comparatively polite I became demanding. Every day Yannev assured me as chairman of BAC that the Spassovs and the rest of the Orion Group were going to repay their debts, begging me to be patient for just one more day. It never happened.

Once I was involved in the day-to-day running of the bank I saw at first hand how things operated. One morning a young man came to see me. He told me he had already borrowed some money from the bank and wanted to increase the loan. He was full of great plans for his business. I told him we would be happy to lend him more money, and explained the conditions of repayment.

'Rest assured that your ten per cent will not be forgotten,' he said, with a conspiratorial wink.

Fighting it Out

'You stupid boy!' I shouted, my rage boiling over. 'Do you seriously think I would steal from my own bank?'

Obviously that was exactly what he thought, and why wouldn't he? It was what everyone else was doing. I threw him out of the building, feeling close to despair. How could I hope to fight against corruption when it was so endemic to the system?

The corruption of that young man, however, was nothing compared to what was going on at a higher level. Later, when it became government policy to privatise many of the big nationalised industries, it was a field day for the crooks. To begin with, the government would simply give huge chunks of industry away to their friends or relatives. In other cases managers of enterprises would deliberately run them down in order to decrease their value, and then buy them for themselves. They would come to see me to borrow the money for their purchases, proudly boasting about what they had done.

'You are so dumb,' became my usual answer to these delegations. 'You've ruined something that cost four billion dollars, and now you want another eight billion dollars to put it back together. You must think I'm as stupid as you. Get out!'

Another example of this insanity came in 1997 when one of my employees, who ran a metals trading company for me called Daru Metal, brought a man to me in Vienna. He was a national trade union boss and boasted that the prime minister did everything he told him. One of the metallurgical combines this man controlled had 25,000 workers on the payroll and was producing huge steel plates in mighty smelting works.

After a few preliminaries they told me that together we could buy this entire combine for one dollar.

'But it's worth billions,' I protested.

'Exactly,' they said proudly, 'but it needs modernising and the government wants that to be done with private money. They're willing to forgive a few million in debts if the sale goes ahead.'

The Great National Robbery

'We don't have the capability to do that sort of work,' I said.

'We don't have to,' they replied, as if I was stupid. 'The combine owns twenty hotels and some land along the Black Sea coast, plus some other assets. We would sell off those assets and then hand the rest back to the government, admitting we can't fulfil our obligations.'

'Absolutely not,' I said. 'I don't want to be the man who asset-strips what was left of Bulgaria's industrial past.'

They left the office, obviously thinking I was a fool.

A few months later I read that a company called 'Daru Metals' (notice the extra s) had done the deal. I immediately contacted every government office I knew to explain that this was a phoney company and that I had nothing to do with the deal, whatever they might have been told. I did not receive a single reply from anyone; the deal went ahead and more of the country's money disappeared into fraudulent private hands.

Despite everything, I remained determined throughout to persevere with my investments in Bulgaria. I had been a thorn in their side and their power to frustrate me was formidable. I was already the exclusive importer of BMWs and when BMW bought Rover in 1994 we came to an agreement to build a factory for the assembly of Rover cars in Varna. It was to be a joint company, with 51 per cent going to BMW and 49 percent to my various companies, including BAC. We chose to manufacture the Maestro, because it had the simplest design and mechanics; it had proved its durability and strength, and agreed to start assembling Rover's newer models at a later date. This was a first for Bulgaria; we had never constructed our own automobiles before. It meant many new jobs, and work for a huge number of subcontractors. More importantly it meant the transfer of skills into the country. Usually such deals are the result of negotiations between governments, but we managed to

Fighting it Out

do it on our own, with no help from the authorities. This was a deliberate policy, since we didn't want to become involved with any parts of the Orion Group, knowing they would be siphoning off money through bribes, theft and corruption. As a result of our independent stance, the communist government was determined to destroy the enterprise.

Their first step was to prohibit all directors of state companies, as well as private companies under the guardianship of the communists, from buying cars from us, thus artificially narrowing the market. Then they refused to give us any tax preferences or to exclude parts from customs duties, concessions that would be automatic in any other country trying to attract investment from abroad. Then Bulgaria's deputy prime minister travelled to England to visit Rover, and told the management there that they should replace us with the Orion Group. The process started but when BMW got wind of what was going on they fired those who were conspiring with the Bulgarian government against a long-standing business partner. Finally, we were declared national enemies and traitors to Videnov's government and Rover left the country.

It's my experience that big business is based on trust as much as money. If you don't trust your partner, whether it's a company, a state or an individual, no amount of money can make a deal work. By chasing away a partner like Rover, the government showed other potential investors that nothing had changed in Bulgaria, destroying any hope of attracting any significant investments to the country.

By changing the Bulgarian Communist Party to the Bulgarian Socialist Party the old semi-literate communists from the forties were replaced by neo-communists from the Komsomol. These people were just as dogmatic and narrow-minded as the rulers of my youth, but where there had been a great deal of idealism amongst the early communists, there was none among the neo-communists. Where once there had been a naïve belief in communist theories, even some morals, the heirs of communism were entirely cynical, a generation of vulgar monsters raised entirely by the Bulgarian Communist Party. They had developed their characters in a rotten society where perceptions of morals, of vocation, of good and evil, beauty and ugliness had been distorted and deformed beyond recognition; a society in which there was no room for a single human virtue. Changing the name did not change the party membership or their way of thinking. The country's foreign debts rose from around three billion to nearly ten billion dollars, and the difference disappeared to the accounts of the chosen ones.

Behind the scenes Andrei Lukanov and Alexander Lillov were losing their power. The practices that Lukanov had set in motion for plundering the country when he was Prime Minister had taken on a life of its own. Men like Spassov, who he had put in place to run the Orion Group, realised they no longer needed his backing and transferred their allegiance to Videnov. I liked Lukanov despite his past and I believed that he might be able to help me put a stop to this robbery which was set to bring Bulgaria to its knees. I arranged a number of meetings with him and he seemed to share my pessimism for the future.

'Videnov and his people cannot be influenced by any reasonable argument,' he eventually decided. 'They should simply be removed.'

I agreed with him and felt that if anyone could achieve it, it was a wily old fox like Lukanov. But then I heard that Videnov wouldn't even have a meeting with him. It seemed Lukanov's access to power had slipped away. Where once he had been the most powerful man in the country, with no opposition, he now couldn't even get an audience with the prime minister. His

Fighting it Out

courage, however, remained in tact and he started talking in parliament and in the papers about how he intended to bring Videnov down. He was signing his own death warrant. Three months later he would be killed.

I also made contact with Lukanov's colleague, Alexander Lillov. He too was worried about the madness that seemed to be infecting the leadership of the party and the way in which the Orion Group was usurping power.

'I feel partly responsible,' he admitted. 'I'm afraid I was one of the people who nurtured Videnov and his circle. But in 1992 nobody wanted to take charge of the party, everyone who knew anything was frightened of the way things were going. All the competent people had disappeared; only Videnov agreed to stay on.'

I could believe that. Videnov had had the look of a man who didn't quite realise what he was getting into the first time I had met him. When I told Lillov I believed the Bulgarian Socialist Party could not survive much longer in its present corrupt form he fell back onto all the old communist clichés of 'bright futures, five-year plans, seven-year plans', and assured me time would heal the wounds. It was hopeless; there was no one else to believe in. Videnov's Komsomol team had total power now, with nothing to constrain them, with a majority in parliament and in the executive. They didn't waste a second in declaring war on their own nation, virtual economic genocide. Lukanov had put the whole structure in place for them, all they had to do was milk it for all it was worth.

There have been campaigns of greater ferocity in history, where whole countries and states have been conquered and leaders killed but where ordinary people have still been left with room for spiritual and material existence, if only because the new leaders needed followers. But the neo-communists had no such long-term strategies. They were on an invisible rampage of looting, willing to destroy everything, taking the very shirts off the backs of their own people. They didn't give a damn for the future of their people or their country.

So, when does a bunch of basic criminals change from being a gang to a 'mafia'? The answer would seem to me to be when they've acquired enough wealth and power to get inside the legitimate structures of local and national government. Criminals might accumulate their primary capital through theft, extortion, murder, blackmail, illegal gambling, prostitution and drug dealing, but they move onto a different plane once they cooperate with one another and become 'organised crime'. The Orion Group started by stealing through puppets like Yannev at BAC but he was one of many. Once the communists came to power the most eminent members of the Orion Group were rewarded with ministerial positions. They in turn appointed people they could trust and started bribing, threatening, blackmailing and corrupting incumbent civil servants. Within a very short time they had made themselves invincible. They were totally in control and able to operate with impunity, out of the sight of the man in the street.

An ordinary man will seek protection against crime from the Ministry of Home Affairs. But if that department is under the control of the mafia, what hope does he have? He is like a lamb going to visit the wolf to ask for assistance against the fox. Jan Videnov might have been able to put it all right if he had acted quickly enough to destroy what Lukanov had started, but the cancer spread so fast it was soon impossible to tell the diseased parts of the body from the healthy areas. Instead, he developed a classic mafia state, imagining it would allow him to rule for ever.

Jan was a typical Komsomol boy, mediocre in every way. As a young man he had established Che Guevara clubs in his native town of Plovdiv. Once in politics he concentrated all his efforts on impressing his superiors in the party. Since blind obedience and unquestioning personal fidelity are always preferred by communists to any other attributes, he soon got noticed. The higher he got the more he surrounded himself with party activists, elementary populists and liars, a gang of thugs with no concept of public service. Once in government they immediately thought they owned everything in the state and commandeered the Bulgarian National Bank, the Ministry of Finance, the National Assembly, the police and every other institution in the country. These people had but one objective: to turn political power into economic power. They believed they could manage with one economic political bureau, but they were not business people and they didn't understand the free market they were planning to exploit. They were doomed to fail, and in the course of failing they would destroy everything that was left.

Now that I had discovered what was going on, I could see the scam against the banks was very simple. They had a list of people who were allowed unlimited credit at the state and private banks that were run by puppets like Yannev. Anybody not on the list would not be eligible for credit. I insisted on creating a credit committee at BAC comprised of specialists, in order to review all applications for credit. Yannev was constantly insisting on checking the names on 'the list', which he kept in his safe.

'What list?' I asked naïvely at the beginning. 'Is it a list of people who've not repaid previous credits?'

He was evasive at first but eventually had to admit it was a list of 'our people' attached to fictitious companies whose only purpose was to receive millions of dollars in cash and then go bankrupt or into liquidation, the money having disappeared abroad. Alternatively, they would sell their companies to criminals, people who could never be forced to repay debts, who would kill debt collectors without a second thought.

In the spring of 1995 the bank was finally forced to fire

The Great National Robbery

Yannev and a few weeks later he was arrested at the airport attempting to leave the country. The newspapers said the arrest was at my insistence, but it was not true; we had not filed any complaints against him at that stage. Later, prosecutors came to ask for our cooperation and it became obvious they had been watching him for some time. We gave them the documents they required but they had already amassed a great deal of information.

When Zhivkov was running the country, from 1954 to 1989, Yannev had been executive director of Litex Bank in the Lebanon, the only Bulgarian bank abroad. He got himself into trouble for misusing his official position and was prosecuted in the eighties. Mircho Spassov intervened in order to save his life, but obviously at a price. From then on Yannev had to do whatever Spassov, his family and cronies wanted. He became the Spassovs' advocate, refusing to hear a bad word about them, and allowed them to remove millions from the banking system.

By the time the Bulgarian people woke up to what was happening it was too late; the communists controlled every position in the country, including the national bank. Although they were doubtless pleased to see my money coming into the country, the would-be robbers were clearly made uncomfortable by my physical presence. My name was not on any lists of favoured people. I was not part of any scheme and they must have been able to see very quickly that I was unlikely to want to join with them in their plots. They must have heard me pleading for ethical behaviour in public life and known I'd be their enemy. Almost as soon as I arrived they probably decided I needed to be got rid of. One way to get rid of me would be to destroy BAC. What they didn't realise was that by destroying BAC, which was seen as the most stable and trustworthy private bank in the country, they would set off a domino effect in the banking sector which would quickly spread and cause the collapse of the whole system.

CHAPTER FIFTEEN

THE DESTRUCTION OF THE BANKS

A few days before Christmas 1995, the director of Dobrudjanska Bank, which BAC owned, called me.

'Boss,' he said, 'there are some men going from house to house telling people to withdraw their money from the bank because we're going to go bankrupt.'

'What people?' I wanted to know. 'Who sent them?'

'God knows,' he said. 'What shall we do?'

'Try to find out who they are,' I said, 'and make sure nothing is going wrong at the bank.'

I knew that Dobrudjanska was one of the strongest banks in the country, but I had no idea how successful these people would be at convincing customers this wasn't the case. Over Christmas the bank was closed so there was no way of judging what was going to happen, and no way of retaliating. We simply had to wait until everything opened again after the holiday in order to assess the damage the campaign might be doing. It gave our enemies even longer to go about their malicious work. On the face of it, it seemed absolute madness for them to be setting out to finally destroy the bank – killing the goose that laid the golden egg. But since I had been making

Fighting it Out

things difficult they were no longer able to plunder from the bank on the same scale. Also, their policies were, throughout, always very much for the short term; they had an inclination that life in Bulgaria could not always go on this way, and knew that their days were numbered.

As soon as the Christmas festivities were over and everyone was back at work the same director rang me again. 'Their plan's working,' he said. 'There's panic. Customers are queuing up to take their money out.'

Other people began phoning me, telling me to tune into the radio or brought newspapers into the office for me to see. They all told the same story: Dobrudjanska was going bankrupt. Within days the most stable provincial bank in the country was in liquidation and the rumours that had been so deliberately spread became a reality. The financial impact on BAC was minimal, but the message was clear: this was a dress rehearsal; we would be next on their hit list. These people were experts in the use of propaganda. They were skilled in dirty tricks and creating panic was one of them.

I realised that the plotters must already be at work, but I had no way of counteracting whatever they might be doing until they came out into the open. All we could do was continue to go about our business and wait to see what they would do. The first rumblings came in a parliamentary debate. Zlatomir Orsov, an MP, an active member of the Orion Group stood up before the elected representatives with a worried look on his face, and expressed his concern about the state of BAC.

Simply by saying those words he had created a story the newspapers could follow up on. They didn't bother to check the facts; if they had they would have discovered that BAC was in an extremely healthy state. Despite the bad credit Yannev had allowed the bank to give out, there was a huge amount of capital moving through; more than enough to cover our obligations. Another MP added his voice to Orsov's, and then the chief editor of the communist newspaper Zemya. We were determined not to panic and continued to work as if nothing was wrong, but the newspapers were beginning to use phrases like 'the indisputable facts', while still not troubling themselves to check anything with us. The television and radio stations were also reporting the supposed traumas going on behind the scenes at BAC.

I was well aware of the power of television to damage us in the eyes of the public. There was one particular show that kept inviting on the crooks who had got their hands on our money and interviewed them as if they were genuine business people. They sat in the studio, looking like innocent lambs, complaining about me and how I had cold-heartedly tried to retrieve BAC's money by destroying their worthy little companies. They had power but I had money, which made me a threat. To consolidate their power they had to strip me of my money. The show was such a success that it became something of a nightly soap opera, with me as chief villain.

Rumen Spassov himself made an appearance, explaining how I was stealing from my own bank. The mafia were both my prosecutors and my judges. In the face of the power which these men held, and the strings that they could pull within the corrupt network behind the scenes, I had no recourse to law to combat this slander. They stole the nation's money and then claimed to be its saviours. The communists had once again come to power by promising the people riches, and were now stripping them of all they had. Kamen Toshkov, a member of the Orion Group, also appeared on national television in his capacity as the boss of the banks' supervisory commission of BNB and was a significant figure in orchestrating the campaign against me. A man that senior would only have taken orders directly from the prime minister.

'We're concerned about the state of affairs in BAC,' he said. 'They've had some problems, but I believe they'll cope.'

Fighting it Out

With those few words of faint praise he damned BAC to destruction, just as he intended. The next morning thousands of people beseiged every branch of the bank the moment we opened for business. We had plenty of assets to pay everyone, but the panic didn't subside and the frenzy was fed by media reports of what was happening. People who hadn't believed the rumours saw pictures of the queues and decided leaving their money in BAC was not a risk worth taking.

I contacted the television stations and said I wanted to make a statement in my capacity as chairman of the board of directors and owner of the bank. Within an hour there was an official in my office informing me that such a move would not be allowed. They could say whatever they wanted about me on air, but I was not allowed to respond. An enterprising young journalist managed to get to me to do an interview, which somehow got broadcast despite the decree from on high, albeit in a form so heavily edited even I couldn't make out what I was saying. The girl was fired the moment the interview went out.

Over the following few days customers continued to come into the banks and we gave them their deposits without any argument. They saw we weren't trying to slam the door in their faces and the panic began to subside. It looked as if we might be able to survive the run. But orders must then have gone out to finish us off. They were obviously tired of fighting; they wanted me removed with no more fuss. A television crew filmed the last of a queue in front of one of our smaller branches and that evening, on prime time news, they made the announcement.

'BAC has collapsed!'

If we had had orderly queues until then, the following morning our branches were surrounded by angry mobs, their worries fed by infiltrators who moved amongst them spreading new rumours. There's no bank in the world that can survive if every depositor decides to withdraw their savings at the same time. We were doomed, and so was the Bulgarian banking system. At this stage BNB should have agreed to back us until the crisis had passed, since one of the main tasks of a central bank is to give short-term credits and deposits to commercial banks. Every time I went to meet the bank's head, Todor Vultchev, I was greeted with smiles, coffee and promises that 'Tomorrow everything will be settled,' but the next day things would be just the same and nothing would happen.

People working within BNB told me that if I would agree to a three or four per cent bribe, they could settle the additional funding problem. I declined their kind offer. Is it possible to imagine officials of the Bank of England making such an offer to a private banker? If I had accepted we might have saved the bank, but we would have joined the plotters, our hands would have been as dirty as theirs and I would have become part of the great Bulgarian tradition of bribery.

English advisers I had brought in from KPMG, one of the biggest auditing companies in the world, to help me build the bank, suggested I loan more of my own money to BAC, thereby raising the capital and decreasing the relative share of the money stolen. I agreed and we signed contracts and papers. I deposited six and half million dollars into a Swiss bank in readiness, with me as the only signatory. I knew that if anyone else within BAC could sign for the money it would be gone within hours.

We wrote letters to BNB asking for permission to use this money, but received no replies. We had investments that would cover the money being demanded by depositors, but we had given long-term credit that prevented us from gaining access to those investments. We were finally running out of liquidity and time. The hysteria grew and when BNB finally made a gesture by giving us a modest allowance, the money sank like water in sand. Still I refused to give up. Todor Vultchev had been replaced at BNB and I thought we might stand a chance with

Fighting it Out

a fresh approach. The people from KPMG prepared a new protection strategy with schedules and tables and I took them to meet the new leadership at BNB. The English consultants patiently explained how they believed BNB could stabilise the financial system before it melted down completely, but it soon became obvious that these senior civil servants had been ordered to destroy us.

They paid lip service to our pleas by giving BAC one billion levs in February 1996 (something in the region of $10 million at the time), bringing our total debt to them to two and a half billion levs. Compared to our balance of more than fifty billion at that time it was nowhere near enough, but it was something. The loan was given before lunch on a Friday and in the afternoon a courier arrived from BNB to tell me the directors had changed their minds.

'If you cannot return the money by Monday, you're obliged to give BAC to BNB as a gift.'

He handed me a letter to show this had been officially sanctioned. I asked for a postponement. I had another idea. I'd made contact with Ivan Kostov who was leader of the opposition party, the Union of Democratic Forces (UDF). Later he was to become Prime Minister. (His wife was secretary of the former Communist Party so the cancer lived on.) He agreed to meet me, but not only did the meetings have to be kept secret, they had to be held 2,500 metres up a mountain in the middle of winter.

'You're the official leader of the opposition,' I protested. 'What are you afraid of?'

'These are dangerous times,' he said. 'I can't risk them seeing us together.'

We had several of these high altitude meetings, at which I shared everything I knew about the Orion Group and their misuse of power. He organised his own team of investigators who confirmed everything I had told him and there were several debates in the national assembly on the activities of the Orion Group.

'The Orion Group,' Jan Videnov replied when questioned in parliament, 'are my friends and are very respectable people.'

I felt there were some decent people in the UDF who could be trusted and I suggested to Kostov that I give the bank to the party.

'All private banks in Bulgaria are in the hands of the communists one way or another,' I argued. 'It gives them all the economic power. I don't believe I can save BAC because there are too many people against me, but the bank is still sound and the UDF could manage and protect it. It works hand in glove with the best insurance company in the country.' He understood what I was saying and called meetings of the UDF immediately. I heard his reply on national television, turning down my proposal. In private he assured me that once he was in power he would prosecute all the people who had destroyed the country. Those prosecutions have still not taken place.

The communists had done more than just defraud the banking system; they had sold all of Bulgaria's grain reserves and stolen the profit, arousing the starving people to riot in the streets, events which eventually brought Kostov to power in January 1997. He promised the public he would prosecute everyone involved in that fraud as well, but the people are still waiting to see any justice.

Throughout all of this I had been struggling to recover some of the money which had been siphoned from BAC via Yannev. One of the heaviest debts was the forty million German marks owed by Slavtchev, a puppet for the Orion Group, who had passed the money straight on to Spassov. Yannev had given him the money without guarantees and I undertook a number of measures, including the confiscation of his organisation, Agropromstroi, to guarantee the debt. The organisation had bought huge agricultural companies. It had trucks, factories and lands. This was as early on as 1995, but although the

Fighting it Out

confiscation was all done legally, I must have interfered with the interests of someone very powerful because a few weeks later, in the autumn of 1995, I received my first written threat.

It read: 'This hereby confirms the sentence of the chief Revolutionary Tribune against the people's enemy – the fascist Atanas Tilev. Conditions for the cancellation of this sentence are to give back to the working people in the form of donations the amount of two billion, four hundred million levs, including the donation of the Agropromstroi company to the municipality of Mihailovgrad.'

These 'official' threats were followed up by 'unofficial' notes, unsigned, and clearly the work of hired thugs. It was only a few months after the first letter that I received another death sentence: 'We inform you that a sentence has been passed against you.' Underneath was written; 'Death to Fascism – Money for the Workers'. Shortly afterwards I received a further note in the same vein, but adding 'this is also applicable to seven of your closest relatives.'

The inference has always been that I, a capitalist, was draining the country of its money. On paper I had a salary that was enormous by Bulgarian standards, but I never drew a single lev of it. I had to have it so that my subordinates could have higher salaries, but anything that was left after the payment of taxes was donated to a local orphanage. I had a secretary whose full time job was to liaise with the orphanage to find out what they needed each month. I knew it would be pointless simply giving them money, since someone in the management would steal it or spend it on cars, trips and meals, so we would buy them clothes or washing machines or whatever they asked for, and ensured it was delivered. That was where my salary went each month. How could I have lived with myself if I had been taking money out of a country so poor? My aim was to help create national wealth, not take it for myself.

I never went to the orphanage personally; I didn't want any

The Destruction of the Banks

glory or gratitude. Charity can easily be defiled. Many of the big bosses' wives in Bulgaria have taken up fashionable charities, and their husbands blackmail people into giving money with lines like, 'Unless you support my wife's charity you will not have your licence renewed'.

In my innocence I wrote a complaint to the Minister of Home Affairs about the death sentences, enclosing the letters and hoping for a little protection. I later discovered the minister was handing the letters directly on to the people who had issued them, the people who had labelled me an oppressor and an exploiter and had set the former officers of the security services and police onto me.

A single issue of a magazine called *Poslé* (Afterwards), came out, carrying an anonymous piece entitled 'Brigo Karlovitch Tilev' (a combination of the names of my friend Brigo, who was by then chief of intelligence services, Lukanov and myself), accusing us of plotting a coup against Videnov. The magazine was circulated to members of Parliament, newspapers, banks, official institutions and shops. I'm told it was published by the department of analysis of the Ministry of Home Affairs, conceived, developed and published by the government, using public money.

In 1996 one of my directors was kidnapped as he was getting into his car outside his house. He and his family had been under constant threat and there had been several attempts at blackmail. Now they were demanding a ransom of $2 million. I did everything I could to free my man, trying not only the regular police, but also trying to see if private security groups might be able to free him. Surrendering and paying up the ransom money was not an option – it was against my policy, and would, anyway, only have led to further kidnappings. My efforts were to no avail. A month later they brought him back drugged beyond recognition and completely devastated. They might just as well have killed him since they

Fighting it Out

had effectively put an end to his life in every other way.

I hired a great many more bodyguards to cover me and my daughter Maria, who was living with me and attending a local school, and ordered an armour-plated car. We installed metal detectors and guards on all the entrances to the bank. It seemed I had to take things more seriously.

I made one last visit to the chief of BNB in March the same year.

'Do you realise what you're doing?' I asked, going on to describe the ramifications for the economy if he allowed BAC to go under, taking the rest of the banking system with it.

'What can I do?' he asked, spreading his hands, which were shaking like leaves in the breeze. 'The orders come from above, from the highest places.'

I shrugged. 'There is nothing more I can do. I want you to write down that at this moment I give you everything; but I want you to promise you will at least keep the bank intact and give the money back to the people to whom it belongs.

A journalist came to see me the next day. When she came into my office she expressed surprise not to find me with an ice pack on my forehead, planning to jump from the roof.

'I'm not so foolish that I would risk everything I own in one country,' I admitted. 'It's my philosophy always to ensure that I have a back door to escape through should a business go wrong. It's a primary rule of business never to start a venture until you're sure you're able to afford the downside.'

'But the whole Bulgarian banking system is collapsing,' she said. 'Doesn't that worry you?'

'Of course it worries me for the Bulgarian people,' I replied. 'But it's not the end of the world for me. If the American, British and Swiss banking systems started collapsing then I might start to worry for myself.'

Two years later, in 1998, Todor Vultchev, the former head of BNB, gave an interview on Radio Free Europe.

The Destruction of the Banks

'Maybe this crisis would not have been reached if people close to the government had not said that the banks were closing one after another,' he admitted. 'If we had not been stopped from supporting some banks and if the BAC had not been left to collapse? I dare say, quite objectively, this would not have happened if it had not been for purely political reasons, since Mr Tilev had to be hit because of the interests of other groups. But the boomerang effect was underestimated and it was not taken into account that the collapse of one bank cannot happen in isolation.'

After I had presented BNB with BAC, which I thought was what they wanted, I rang my children and suggested meeting them for a skiing holiday. My nerves were in shreds. I thought, now that I had given them everything they wanted, they would leave me alone. But the order for my arrest was already in the computers of GKPP – the Bulgarian domestic Secret Service.

To this tempestuous period of my life I must record a disillusioning footnote. In 1995, while I was sadly forced to witness my countrymen destroying themselves and their country, I was trying to think of something else to do. I saw a map of the world distribution of a product called Basilicum Bulgaricum. This is the bacteria from which every yoghurt in the world is manufactured, and it all comes from Bulgaria. A company called Bulgaricum holds the licence and the bacteria has to be exported to customers every two weeks, otherwise it dies and they can no longer make yoghurt. It's a wonderful company with a worldwide patent that is Bulgaria's equivalent to Coca-Cola.

I noticed on the map that China was blank; one of those white spots that always seem to attract me. No yoghurt was being made anywhere in China. Since virgin territories and communist regimes are my speciality, I bought up the yoghurt rights for the whole of the country. I then formed a joint venture with the All China Association of Milk Producers.

Fighting it Out

They would provide the land and some broken-down buildings and I would supply the best equipment in the world, importing it from Italy and Germany.

The project went ahead and we built the most advanced factory of its type on earth. After a big inauguration ceremony with ministers and ambassadors in attendance, we started manufacturing. It was a huge success. There were queues in the supermarkets and we made plans for building more factories all over the country. It looked like it was going to produce billions of dollars a year for us.

Seven months after the opening I received a call from my manager in China. 'Boss,' he said, 'the Chinese have stolen the money for the trucks.'

I had sent over $150,000 to buy a fleet of trucks.

'They've stolen it?' I was incredulous.

'Yes,' he said, 'and they've gone. They've closed the factory and gone off to do it themselves somewhere else.'

'But they can't do it without us,' I protested.

'They've gone,' he repeated. He too was obviously finding it hard to understand why anyone would destroy a business that had the potential to make billions for the sake of a few dollars in cash.

I sent him to see everyone I could think of, every government minister and foreign ambassador in the country. No one was interested. He found a Chinese lawyer who had trained at Harvard who pressed the Chinese in their own language. Within days the lawyer had secret service men in his office telling him to drop the case or he would end up dead. There was nobody left to go to. It seems that it is Chinese state policy to lure in foreign companies and then steal their money and equipment. Because they are not members of the World Trade Organisation you can't sue them. All you can do is go to arbitration in Switzerland, which is what I did. But how will I enforce the findings if they are in my favour?

The Destruction of the Banks

Communist nations seem to go through a series of destinct phases. It comes to power through the revolutionary zeal of a handful of idealists – true beleivers who act in good faith and are able to persuade those around them of the validity of their cause. The next stage is suppression: the natural and historic free market tendencies of a people need to be stamped out and a highly authoratarian government is needed to impose the communist ideologies and try to put them into practice. This leads to a system of strict law and order. The next stage is plunder: Out of this near absolute authoritarianism, powerful individuals start to pilfer, using their position for their own personal gain. This leads, inevitably, to a mafia system: a network of corrupt individuals whose only interest is to perpetuate the system as it stands so that they can continue to reep their unjust rewards. At some point this whole system simply implodes – the country collapses. China, in the account I have just given, stands now at the same communist stage as Russia.

As a venture capitalist, an entrepreneur and an investor, I constantly have to make decisions about what businesses to back and what to avoid. The sensible thing, of course, would be to invest everything in property and sleep beautifully every night, but that is not an attractive prospect; it does not stir the soul. What one really wants is to find is something that is revolutionary and benefits mankind, to be first at something, and then to reap the financial rewards of that triumph.

All business is gambling, because only one person can win a contract or make a sale, and there is never a definite way to predict who the winner will be. All you can do to operate as safely as possible is research the environment and competitive situation. Everyone will always promise the sky; and the businessman has to assess whether the promises are achievable, and then gamble on his judgement. In China I had gambled and lost.

CHAPTER SIXTEEN

"MR TILEV MUST BE HIT"

The first order for my arrest under spurious charges of corruption came in March 1996 and was signed by the chief of national police, Ivan Dimmov, who had been given his job as a reward for his work as driver and personal bodyguard to Rumen Spassov. It had no legality, but that didn't mean he wouldn't enforce it.

Dimmov sent telegrams to all the airports and border points ordering that I be restrained from leaving the country. When I heard the news I was furious, although I didn't yet feel in imminent danger of arrest. I fought with Dimmov for three days and nights, creating as much of a hoo-ha as I could. In the end they cancelled the order and let me out. I travelled for four months and returned in July of that year. I had invested a lot of money and lot of myself in Bulgaria. It was my homeland. I couldn't turn my back on it. I didn't feel guilty about anything that had happened and I didn't have any debts, I hadn't stolen anything or killed anyone. I was not going to be forced out that easily.

While I was travelling the mafia had appointed their own people to run BAC and had given them the task of writing complaints and making false statements about me, to discredit me, to prove my guilt and their innocence. Their reports were a tissue of lies and inventions.

They had by no means finished with me. After spending a passable summer in Varna and on my way out of the country once more in August 1996, I was arrested on an order signed personally by the chief of National Security Services, and taken back under guard, just like a spy or criminal. This was still not legal and I was soon free again, but it had more weight than Dimmov's attempt. It began to occur to me that being arrested under the right authority might be the way they could bring me down. The thought worried me.

In 1997 I sued the police and counter intelligence for wrongful arrest, not because I wanted revenge, but because I wanted to show the world how far the mafia's tentacles had reached. Five years later I was awarded one dollar in damages. The time it took to win was ludicrous and the amount derisory, but at least it shows judges in Bulgaria are not running scared any more, not at the moment. They certainly were at the time of my arrest.

After Yannev was arrested at the airport in 1995 trying to leave the country, his brand new Argentinian passport in his pocket, more journalists started to show an interest in the activities of the Orion group. It seemed the scales were finally dropping from their eyes. Yannev's links with the Group began to become clearer. Revealing documents started to appear, but still no one was held responsible for the death sentences imposed on me; no one was punished.

'They're not going to be writing you any more letters,' I was told by a contact.

'Thank God for that,' I said.

'It's worse,' he said. 'They've hired an assassin.'

'Do we know who my executioner is?' I asked.

'We do. Shall we alert the police?'

'No.' I had no faith in the authorities any more. 'I'll handle

'Mr Tilev Must be Hit'

it. Find out where this man works from.'

With the collapse of the Soviet Union and the pretence at democracy in Bulgaria, the government had lost the power to use secret police to do its dirty work. Where once they had had 'wet squads' whose sole job was to kill, they no longer had the ability to force people to murder or intimidate to order. To fill this vacuum they had created a new criminal class, using many of the thousands of athletes who had been trained in communist times to compete for the glory of communism and who were now unemployed. These men, many of them champions in karate and boxing and deprived of their comfortable state salaries, were only too happy to take whatever work was offered to them. Some of my own bodyguards, for example, were championship rowers.

The man who had been hired to kill me was a well known wrestler. We found out where his office was and I paid him a visit with one of my directors and two of my bodyguards. He leapt to his feet as we exploded into the room. He had obviously expected me to wait patiently for him to kill me, not to come looking for him. He didn't seem to know what to say. He blustered, talking about himself in the plural, as if he was part of the establishment.

'We've heard a lot about you,' he spluttered. 'We know what you've been doing.'

I snapped back, 'We've heard that you've received orders to kill me!'

He was obviously not a clever man and quickly confessed. 'But I intended to talk to you first, to clear up any conflict before I did the job.'

'Let me explain something to you,' I hissed. 'If anything happens to me or to anyone close to me, I'll be forced to respond in an adequate manner!'

His mouth was hanging open in incomprehension; I was obviously going to have to spell it out for him. 'If one of my children dies, one of yours dies the next day. If something happens to my parents, something happens to yours. Now do you understand?'

I felt I had become one of his kind, but it was the only way I knew how to deal with the situation. If there are no authorities you can appeal to, then you have to fight such people as equals. By the time we left his office he seemed to believe I meant what I said. It didn't occur to him I hadn't the remotest idea where his family were and that, as an international businessman, I was highly unlikely to go around killing people. I'd acted just as he would have done in the circumstances, just as he would have expected anyone in a position of power to act, and so he saw no reason to disbelieve me.

I sent some more people round to see him a few days later and he assured them that he had turned the job down. Informants told me the mafia were looking for someone new. It was turning into a war, albeit a phoney one.

Knowing you are a target for assassins is an unpleasant feeling. You need nerves of steel and a sense of humour. You're on the alert every moment of the day and night. I had surrounded myself with bodyguards, but I knew most of them could be cheaply bought. Indira Gandhi had been killed by one of her own entourage. All I could really hope was that by having enough of them the threshold for killing me would become too high to be worth anyone taking up the challenge. More than my own death, however, I was fearful for my daughter, Maria. If they killed or kidnapped her it would be unbearable. I had twelve men armed with sub-machine guns following her around.

'Anything suspicious and you shoot until nothing moves,' I told them, 'and I'll take care of the explanations.'

The agony lasted from 1993 to 1996. My lady friend wanted me to negotiate with the governing mafia, find a middle path, but I couldn't do it. I knew I was the only independent person left. If I didn't fight them they'd take the whole country. My parents agreed with me. I knew I could die, but I believed that if they succeeded in their plan it would be worse.

The final straw came in August 1996 when I heard that there was a warrant out for my arrest once more, and this time it was legal and official. It had all the right signatures for them to be able to lock me up for a very long time. The death threats I could deal with, but I knew that if the authorities managed to get me into custody I was finished. If they were able to cut me off from the outside world they could do whatever they liked. I would be in as bad a position as if I had been kidnapped by criminals, maybe even worse. At least you can negotiate with kidnappers. They could hold me in custody for virtually as long as they liked, and by the time I got out I would be a broken man, physically, spiritually and possibly also financially. That was the moment when I decided it was time to leave the country by whatever means possible before they came to get me, and so I came to be walking across the border in thirty-five-degree temperatures, forced to escape from my own country.

CHAPTER SEVENTEEN

SO WHAT NOW?

By the time others in the party finally woke up to what was going on and removed Videnov from power in January 1997, sending him back to his village, it was too late for Bulgaria. By then the economy had collapsed, the majority of the banks having closed their doors for ever. I, however, was once again free to return to my homeland without fear of arrest.

The great truth that we now know is that communism can only retain power through force. The moment it's defeated the system it leaves behind collapses, with devastating effects on the people. As well as creating economic devastation it also takes away individuality, turning people into a flock of zombies, slaves who have no idea what to do with freedom when it comes.

Despite all my disappointments, I still have dreams for my country. I would like to create a modern farm as an example of what can be done, a close-cycle farm, integrated and super efficient. The problem is getting something like that going in a country like contemporary Bulgaria, without anything being stolen.

Although I have a lot of admiration for many of the UDF

So What Now?

members who are now governing the country, I'm saddened that no one has yet had the strength to punish Videnov and his circle of cronies for what they did to our country, all the crimes which have been neatly grouped under the umbrella description 'inadequate political decisions'. They demolished the banking system, ruined the economy, assassinated an ex-Prime Minister, stole the very bread from the mouths of the people and isolated Bulgaria from the international community, but still they are free to spend their ill-gotten gains.

How is it possible that after the Supreme Court of Appeal ordered Agropromstroi to be handed over to BAC as compensation for the enormous credit that was owed, it is still today in the hands of Borislav Slavchev? The death sentences may not have worked in getting the company returned to him, but the moment I gave BAC to the government Slavchev received Agropromstroi back on behalf of the Orion Group.

There is still no legislation to force people like the Spassovs and Tsetsi to return their stolen millions or to pay for their crimes against so many small depositors.

No one will ever be able to discover just how many billions of dollars were drained during those years and spirited away into Western banks. But however many billions it was, this was only Bulgaria and far greater sums have certainly been siphoned out of Russia and other Eastern Bloc countries by former communist leaders. With the interest they have earned in the West, the communists have probably stolen over a trillion dollars from their people, some of whom are among the poorest on the planet. It has probably been among the biggest and most successful heists in history.

The people investigating the murder of Lukanov have followed the trail to Angel Vassilev, managing director of Colonel, one of the Orion Group companies, and he has been brought back to Sofia from Prague. Vassilev is charged for paying for the hit. It is claimed that it was carried out by his relatives, employees and two Ukrainians. Perhaps the wheels of justice are beginning to turn effectively.

As this narrative is penned, however, changes are at last afoot. My friend, King Simeon II is in power, and in the King, we have an honest and dependable leader who should be able to lead Bulgaria out of this era of institutionalised corruption.

The King and I have known one another for some time, and although his royal blood lends him an innate authority, it is tempered by a natural humility which is endearing to all who come into contact with him.

As Prime Minister of Bulgaria, King Simeon now has a free hand to lead our country out of the collapsed communist state and into a new era.

For my part, I too still have hopes for my homeland, and trust that in this new environment I may once more have a chance to attempt what I aspired to before; to rebuild a nation and establish a working economy for future generations.